# THE JEWISH
## COOKBOOK

# THE JEWISH
## COOKBOOK

### 70 RECIPES CELEBRATING
### AN HISTORIC CUISINE

## JUDY JACKSON

LORENZ BOOKS
LONDON • NEW YORK • SYDNEY • BATH

For Rachel, Rebecca, Noah and Sam

First published by Lorenz Books in 1996

© 1996 Anness Publishing Limited

Lorenz Books is an imprint of
Anness Publishing Limited
Boundary Row Studios
1 Boundary Row
London SE1 8HP

ISBN 1 85967 293 0

A CIP catalogue record for this book
is available from the British Library

*Publisher:* Joanna Lorenz
*Senior Cookery Editor:* Linda Fraser
*In-house Editor:* Anne Hildyard
*Designer:* Siân Keogh
*Photography:* Amanda Heywood, assisted by Vanessa Kellas
*Styling:* Clare Louise Hunt
*Food for Photography:* Elizabeth Wolf-Cohen, assisted by Zoe Keen
*Illustrator:* Madeleine David

Printed in Singapore by Star Standard Industries Pte. Ltd.

ACKNOWLEDGEMENTS
The author would like to thank Stoves plc for their assistance with a gas hob,
Pifco Ltd. and Moulinex Ltd. for supplying slow-cookers which were invaluable
for the recipe testing.

Stoves plc, Stoney Lane, Prestcot, Merseyside L35 2XW

Pifco Ltd. (Russell Hobbs), Failsworth, Manchester M35 OHS

Moulinex Swan Holdings Ltd. Albion Street, Birmingham B1 3DL

NOTES
For all recipes, quantities are given in both metric and imperial measures and,
where appropriate, measures are also given in standard cups and spoons. Follow
one set, but not a mixture because they are not interchangeable.

Standard spoon and cup measurements are level.
*1 tbsp = 15ml, 1 tsp = 5ml, 1 cup = 250ml/8fl oz*

Australian standard tablespoons are 20ml. Australian readers should use 3 tsp in
place of 1 tbsp for measuring small quantities of gelatine, cornflour, salt etc.

Size 3 (medium) eggs should be used unless otherwise stated.

# CONTENTS

# INTRODUCTION

For centuries Jews have moved from country to country, taking their customs and cooking pots with them. The result is that Jewish cuisine, unlike any other, is enormously varied. Observant Jews have always kept to rigid rules, set down in the Bible, about what can and can't be eaten. So wherever they settled they found new foods and adapted them to complement the dishes they already knew.

There are two distinct Jewish groups – one is *Sephardi* (broadly from the Mediterranean, the Middle and Far East), and the other is *Ashkenazi*, (from France, Germany, Russia and Eastern Europe). Sephardi foods include olive oil, peppers and aubergines from Spain, spicy rice from Iraq and Persia and sweet syrupy pastries from Turkey and Greece. Ashkenazi dishes feature carp and goose and desserts such as cheesecake and apple strudel.

What brings the two groups together are the Jewish Festivals and above all the celebration of the end of the working week – the Sabbath (Shabbat). Whatever the style of mid-week eating, on Friday and Saturday everyone sits down together over long and delicious meals. Jewish people adore eating. They rarely simply go out for a drink. To them a celebration always involves food. When a baby is born there is a party. A child reaching adulthood (13 for a boy, 12 for a girl), has a religious ceremony called a *Barmitzvah* or *Batmitzvah* and this, too, is followed by a party which can take months of

planning. 'The Menu' is the main topic of discussion, both before and afterwards. A wedding is even more special and often involves a buffet lunch at the bridegroom's home the day before. A typical Sephardi table would be laden with platters of meat, rice and stuffed vegetables, followed by nut-filled baklava, date pastries and trays of exotic fruits. Strong black coffee or mint tea would complete the meal.

In English there are no special words associated with offering food to guests. In French you say 'Bon Appétit'. Translated into Hebrew, this is 'Be

Te'avon'. Our grandmothers would simply have said "Enjoy". I hope you too will enjoy the dishes I have chosen to represent the mosaic of Jewish cooking.

### THE JEWISH KITCHEN

Most people know that Jews don't eat pork. The dietary laws, (called *Kashrut*, from which the word 'kosher' comes), explain exactly what is permitted. Camels and hares and any part of an 'unclean' animal are not allowed – cows and sheep are. Shellfish and snails are prohibited, while fish with fins and scales can be eaten. Domestic birds like chickens and geese are fine, but birds of prey are not. At the end of a long description in Deuteronomy comes a passage condemning "boiling a kid in its mother's milk". From this comes the idea of not eating any milk or dairy product with meat. So for anyone unfamiliar with the rules, here is an explanation of what to expect.

### INGREDIENTS THAT NEED CARE
### MEAT

Pork, ham and bacon are strictly forbidden and so is any meat from an animal that has not been killed humanely. So meat and poultry must have a 'kosher' label. In most countries only the forequarter of an animal is used so rump steak or leg of lamb are not usually available. Standard products

*Choosing the perfect ingredient at a bustling street market in the Mea She'arim district of west Jerusalem.*

containing even small amounts of meat stock, gelatine or lard are not allowed.

## DAIRY FOOD

Any dairy product like milk, cream or yogurt is never served at the same time, or even just after, a meat meal. So there are no cream sauces with chicken or marinades of lamb in yogurt. After dinner, coffee is served black. After a meat course, cheese is never served.

## FISH

Cod, haddock, herring, mackerel, salmon and sea bass are some of the many fish which are eaten. Monkfish, prawns, lobster, eels and octopus are among those which are not.
Dairy products like cheese can certainly be used with fish and eaten after a meal containing fish.

## EGGS

Eggs are neutral and can be served with either meat, fish or dairy products. It is the custom to break each egg into a cup before stirring it into a mixture, to avoid possible blood spots – a sensible precaution too, in case the egg is bad.

## STOCKS

Home-made stocks can be made from meat, fish or vegetables but chicken or beef stock would never be added to a soup which would later include milk or cream. Kosher meat cubes are available and there is an excellent product to enhance vegetable soups called "Parev (not real) Chicken Stock Powder".

## HIDDEN INGREDIENTS

The accurate labelling of ingredients has encouraged many people to find out more about what they are eating from a health point of view.

Animal fat and gelatine are among the ingredients that observant Jews would avoid, so if you are catering for Jewish friends, it is better to provide totally vegetarian products for them, unless you are buying food from a completely kosher shop.

*Great care is taken in selecting the most perfect specimens of* etrog (*a type of citrus fruit*), *which is one of the items connected with the festival of Succot. This open air market in Jerusalem is specially set up to sell the necessary traditional items used for this festival. The other species used are* aravot (willow), haddasim (myrtles) *and* lulav (palm branch). *Succot is one of the most colourful and happy festivals in the Jewish calendar.*

# INGREDIENTS

### BAGELS
A bagel is a traditional ring-shaped Jewish bread with a golden, shiny crust. Bagels have a dense, chewy texture due to the way they are cooked, which involves boiling them first, then baking. Bagels come plain or with a variety of toppings, including sesame seeds, poppy seeds, onion or garlic. A typical delicatessen snack is bagels filled with cream cheese and smoked salmon, known as *lox*.

### BARLEY
Traditionally eaten as a filling, satisfying food in eastern Europe, barley is now added to slow cooked meat dishes and soups for its delicious, nutty flavour and slightly chewy texture.

### BULGUR WHEAT
This consists of wheat grains which have been partially cooked, dried and crushed, making a grain that is quick to cook. It is used in tabbouleh – a wheat-based salad, and in pilaffs.

### CHALLAH
This classic Jewish yeast bread is made with eggs and has a light, airy texture. It is served on the Sabbath, at holidays and at everyday meals. Although it can

*Clockwise from top left: pitta bread, matzo, matzo crackers, challah, matzo and bagels.*

*A selection of shelled, unshelled and ground nuts, pomegranate and dates*

be made in any size or shape, it often comes in the form of a plaited loaf.

### DATES
A brown, slightly wrinkled fruit with a very sweet flesh. Dates have been eaten since biblical times and they are commonly used today in pastries and breads.

### FLAT NOODLES
Usually made with egg, in addition to flour and water, noodles feature as an accompaniment to many Jewish dishes.

### HONEY
Honey has long been used as a sweetener and in Jewish cooking it is used to make a traditional honey cake for Rosh Hashanah, to ensure the new year will be sweet.

### LENTILS
Red lentils disintegrate during cooking and so are useful thickeners for soup, while the flat grey-green ones retain their texture and colour.

### MATZO
A thin, crisp unleavened bread, made from flour and water, which comes in crackers in various shapes and sizes, it is traditionally eaten during the Passover holiday and can also be used to make dumplings.

### MATZO MEAL
This is available in different textures; medium and fine. It is used for coating foods to be fried, and for dumplings added to chicken soup. The finest texture is used in Passover cakes.

### NUTS
Nuts are widely used in Jewish cuisine. Salted pistachios are often eaten as a nibble before dinner, while chestnuts are added to dishes such as vegetarian cholent and stuffings. Hazelnuts are ground and used instead of flour for desserts and sponges, and pecan nuts are used to decorate brownies. The small creamy coloured pine nut is often toasted and sprinkled over lamb or added to pilaffs. Available whole, flaked or ground, almonds are used in a wide variety of dishes; in desserts, biscuits, flans and included in stuffings for poultry.

### PITTA BREAD
This is a flatbread made with white or brown flour. When warmed, it can be split to form a pocket to stuff with felafel, hummus or salad.

*Clockwise from top left: smatana, tahina, rose water and honey.*

*Clockwise from top left: lentils, flat noodles, barley, vermicelli, matzo meal and bulgur.*

## POMEGRANATE

A large fruit with a leathery red skin, containing hundreds of small seeds, each surrounded by brilliant red, juicy flesh. The seeds are separated by a yellow bitter membrane which is inedible. In Jewish cooking, the pomegranate is squeezed like a lemon for its tart-sweet juice. The juice is used as a marinade for meat, to add flavour and colour.

## ROSE WATER

The essence of rose petals is distilled to a clear liquid, used to perfume desserts and pastries such as baklava.

## SMATANA

A low-fat substitute for soured cream, smatana is used in sauces for sweet or savoury dishes.

## TAHINA

This is a thick, oily paste made from ground toasted sesame seeds that adds a distinctive nutty flavour to hummus. The oil separates out but is easily beaten back into a paste.

## VERMICELLI

Vermicelli is very fine strands of pasta. Known in Jewish cuisine as *lockshen,* it is often added to chicken soup.

# THE JEWISH KITCHEN

### SHABBAT – THE SABBATH

Work is not allowed on Sabbaths or Festivals. Since cooking is considered work – however enjoyable – everything has to be prepared beforehand. So inventive cooks have devised recipes that can be made before Friday evening or left to cook slowly overnight for lunch the next day. For both meals, the table is set with a fine white cloth and the best china and glass. There is always wine and plaited white loaves called *challah.*

Long ago, the centrepiece would be a large stuffed fish (the original gefilte fish) but in hard times when people could no longer afford the whole fish they just used the stuffing and formed it into small balls. These modern gefilte fish balls are often served to begin the meal. Although they used to be made by labourious chopping, now they are made using a food processor.

The best known Shabbat dish is called *cholent.* It is a large casserole full of meat, vegetables and any combination of beans, barley, chick-peas or potatoes. A non-stick frying pan is good for browning the meat first and a slow-cooker will produce a meltingly tender result. Designed for overnight cooking, it is a perfect all-in-one dish for working people.

### EVERYDAY COOKING

Because of the strict separation between milk and meat, observant Jews keep separate utensils, so it is not uncommon to find two complete sets of crockery, saucepans and cutlery in the kitchen.

To compensate for the outlay in kitchen tools, traditional Jewish food is often based on inexpensive fresh ingredients, like fish, vegetables and chicken. Kosher processed and packaged meals are available but they are rarely as good as home-made. The essential ingredients of the dishes I have chosen are time and a love of cooking.

# FESTIVAL FOODS

The foods eaten on each Festival sometimes date back to biblical times. The cycle begins in September. Here is a selection of some of the most appropriate dishes that are served at each Festival.

### ROSH HASHANAH – NEW YEAR
Jewish New Year is not about staying up till midnight and drinking champagne! It is a happy yet serious Festival when sugar or honey are included so that the coming year should be sweet.

Special sweet dishes include:
Turkey breasts with wine and grapes
Apple stuffed duck
Honey cake
Baklava

### YOM KIPPUR – THE DAY OF ATONEMENT
This is a 24-hour fast when no food or drink (even water) is allowed. Naturally great thought goes into what is eaten before and afterwards!

Filling dishes include:
Chicken soup with lockshen
Lamb with lentils and apricots
Fried fish
Home-made pickled cucumbers
Potato salad

*A typical Passover celebration, with symbolic foods telling their story of the oppression of the Jews and their flight from Egypt.*

### TABERNACLES – SUCCOT
For one week in autumn, temporary huts (called *Succot*) are used for eating and even sleeping. It's a reminder of the travels and unstable life of the ancient Israelites in the desert.

Warming meals include:
Barley soup
Golden chicken
Stuffed vegetables
Pear and Almond flan with Chocolate sauce

### CHANUCAH – THE FESTIVAL OF LIGHTS
This winter Festival is a treat for children, with eight days of candle lighting and little presents.

Special fried dishes include:
Falafel with hummus
Potato Latkes
Veal schnitzels with lemon
Pancakes

### PURIM
During this festival a long story is told about the downfall of a wicked enemy, Haman. This is followed by drinks, a great meal and taking small gifts of food to neighbours.

Presents to take include:
Ma-amoul – date pastries
Flaked almond biscuits
Haman's Ears
Chocolate apricots

### PASSOVER
The celebration of Passover dates back to biblical times. The Jews escaped from the tyrannical persecution of the Pharoah in Egypt and left in such haste that their bread dough had no time to rise. The story is retold every year at a special meal called the *Seder*, (which incidentally was being celebrated at the

*The* haggadah – *the book which tells the Exodus story – with wine and matzo.*

Last Supper). The spring festival lasts for eight days. Nothing leavened is eaten and Jewish homes are even cleared of all traces of bread, flour, biscuits and cereals. Matzah (or matzo) which is unleavened bread is eaten instead of bread. The thin crispy squares (or smaller crackers) are sold in packets. Ground matzo meal is used instead of flour.

Cooking for the week is a challenge, but there are such delights as featherweight nut cakes and light-as-air dumplings for soup, called Luft Knaidlach. But to be successful in making some of these dishes, two vital pieces of equipment are required – an electric mixer and blender.

Specialities for Passover include:
Charoset – apple and nut mixture
Chicken Soup with Luft Knaidlach
Matzo Kleis Balls
Roasted Lamb with Courgettes
Chicken Breasts with Burnt Almond Stuffing
Coconut Pyramids
Cinnamon Balls
Jerusalem Artichoke Soup
Halibut in Lemon Sauce
Matzo Pancakes
Hazelnut Sponge with Vanilla Sauce

SHAVUOT – PENTECOST
Seven weeks later in early summer comes the reminder of Moses receiving the Tablets of the Law on Mount Sinai. It's a tradition to eat dairy foods.

Suitable dishes include:
Fresh beetroot with smatana
Smoked salmon parcels
Tomato and red pepper soup
Cucumber and fish salad
Cheesecake

SHABBAT – THE SABBATH
Every Saturday is a day of rest, relaxation and no cooking. The enjoyment comes from eating all the dishes which have been prepared in advance.

Specially good ones include:
Chopped liver with egg and onion
Challa - plaited white bread
Braised beef with vegetables
Beef cholent with hamin eggs

*Special pancakes for Passover, shown here with a delicious savoury topping.*

Slow cooked lamb with barley
Vegetarian cholent
Spicy carrots
Sliced aubergines with garlic and tomato glaze
Red fruit salad
Fruit coulis
Peach kuchen
Cinnamon rolls

# STARTERS
# AND
# SOUPS

The serious business of eating starts before dinner
with bowls of olives, almonds or pistachio nuts.
Some people even crunch whole chilli peppers!
Weekday or special meals often begin with soup.
Since the story of Esau and Jacob who quarrelled
over a bowl of "red pottage", soup has always
been popular. Everyone knows the legendary value
of Chicken Soup. Called "Jewish penicillin" it is
a magical broth that cures all ills and brings
comfort and warmth.

Soups in Eastern Europe had to be thick and
filling in winter, so they often contained lentils,
beans or barley. One version called Krupnik used
dried mushrooms for flavour when meat was scarce.
Nowadays the fashionable dried mushrooms would
be more expensive than the meat!

# Chopped Liver with Egg and Onion

Traditionally, chicken fat was used and the mixture chopped by hand. This modern recipe calls for chicken stock and a blender.

## INGREDIENTS

*Serves 4*
**For the liver pâté**
225g/8oz chicken livers
45ml/3 tbsp oil
1 onion, chopped
45ml/3 tbsp chicken stock

**For the egg and onion**
2–3 eggs, hard-boiled and shelled
2–3 spring onions, chopped
30ml/2 tbsp chicken stock
salt and ground black pepper
olives and gherkins, to serve
red spring onion strips, to garnish

*1* Preheat the grill. Place the chicken livers on an oiled wire rack in a grill pan and cook under the grill for 2–3 minutes on each side.

*2* Heat the oil in a frying pan and sauté the onion until golden. Add the livers and cook briefly, breaking them up with a fork so that they are no longer pink inside. Season.

*3* Add the chicken stock, turn down the heat and continue cooking the liver and onions for a few minutes. Spoon them into a blender or food processor and process until a smooth paste is formed.

*4* To make the egg and onion mixture, put the eggs with the spring onion in the bowl of a blender or food processor. There's no need to wash it first, as it does no harm to flavour the eggs with a little bit of chopped liver. Add the stock, season and blend until smooth.

*5* Serve the chopped liver in a small mound with some of the egg and onion on the side. Serve with olives and gherkins, garnished with red spring onion strips.

# Aubergine Dip

An appetizer to serve with drinks and crisp sticks of raw vegetables. Aubergines are very popular and are almost a staple food in Israel.

## INGREDIENTS

*Serves 4 as a starter or more as a dip*
2 aubergines (about 275g/10oz each)
2 onions, chopped
150ml/¼ pint/⅔ cup olive oil
3 garlic cloves, crushed
juice of 1 lemon
salt and ground black pepper
sprigs of fresh coriander, to garnish
black and green olives, to serve

*1* Preheat the grill. Cut the aubergines in half lengthways and put them on a sheet of foil, skin side up. Grill at least 5cm/2in from the heat for 20 minutes. The skin will start to wrinkle and the flesh will become slightly smoky and soft.

*2* Meanwhile, sauté the onions over medium heat in about 60ml/4 tbsp oil, add the garlic and cook until they are soft but not brown. Season.

*3* Scoop the flesh out of the aubergine halves and put it into a blender with the onion and garlic. Add the lemon juice.

*4* With the blades running, slowly pour in the remaining olive oil to make a very smooth mixture. Taste again for seasoning.

*5* Spoon the dip into bowls. Garnish with sprigs of fresh coriander and serve with black and green olives.

# Falafel

A typical street food in Israel, hot, crisp falafel are served in warm pitta bread.

**INGREDIENTS**

*Serves 4 – makes about 18 small balls*
225g/8oz/1¼ cups dried chick-peas
3 garlic cloves
5ml/1 tsp cumin seeds
5ml/1 tsp coriander seeds
a handful of fresh coriander,
    finely chopped
a handful of flat leaf parsley,
    finely chopped
1.5ml/¼ tsp chilli powder
15ml/1 tbsp lemon juice
5ml/1 tsp salt
5ml/1 tsp baking powder
oil, for deep frying
ground black pepper
pitta bread and hummus, to serve

*1* Soak the chick-peas in water overnight. Drain and discard the water.

*2* Crush the garlic and grind the cumin and coriander seeds with a pestle and mortar. Put the chick-peas in a food processor and process until they are broken up. Add the garlic, spices, fresh herbs, salt and the chilli powder. Process in a blender until smooth.

*3* Add lemon juice, taste for seasoning and add ground black pepper or more spice to taste. Leave to stand for about 30 minutes.

*4* Stir in the baking powder and form the mixture into small balls. Fry in hot oil for a couple of minutes or until the falafel are golden. Drain and serve with pitta bread and hummus.

# Hummus

Traditionally served with falafel, this chick-pea and sesame seed dip is also good with crackers or raw vegetables. The tahina – sesame seed paste – is available from Jewish or Arabic delicatessens. It's worth making twice the quantity as hummus freezes well.

**INGREDIENTS**

*Serves 4 as a starter – more as a dip*
225g/8 oz/1¼ cups chick-peas,
    soaked overnight
115g/4oz/½ cup tahina paste
2 garlic cloves, crushed
juice of 1–2 lemons
60ml/4 tbsp olive oil
salt
cayenne pepper and flat leaf parsley,
    to garnish

*1* Drain the chick-peas and cook in fresh boiling water for 10 minutes. Reduce the heat and simmer for about an hour or until soft. Drain the chick-peas, reserving the cooking liquid.

--- COOK'S TIP ---

If using a can (400g/14oz) of chick-peas, omit the soaking and boiling and follow the instructions from Step 2.

*2* Put the chick-peas into a food processor, add the tahina paste, garlic and a little lemon juice. Process until smooth. Season and add enough cooking liquid to process until creamy. Add more lemon juice or liquid as the hummus stiffens after resting.

*3* Spoon the hummus on to plates, swirl it with a knife and drizzle with olive oil. Sprinkle with cayenne pepper and garnish with parsley.

# Mushroom Pâté

A vegetarian alternative to chopped liver. Frying the onion in butter gives a rich flavour, but you can use oil instead.

## INGREDIENTS

*Serves 4*
30ml/2 tbsp olive oil or butter
2 onions, chopped
350g/12oz/4½ cups mushrooms, chopped or roughly sliced
225g/8oz/1 cup ground almonds
a handful of parsley, stalks removed
salt and ground black pepper
flat leaf parsley, for garnish
thin slices of toast, cucumber, chicory and celery sticks, to serve

*1* Heat the olive oil or butter in a frying pan and sauté the onions over moderate heat until golden. Keep stirring the onions as you fry them. Take care not to burn the butter as it takes a few minutes for the onions to turn opaque and then start to brown.

*2* Add the mushrooms and continue frying until the juices start to run. Season well.

*3* Put the fried onion and mushrooms into a blender or food processor with the juices. Add the ground almonds and parsley and process briefly. The pâté can either be smooth or you can leave it slightly chunky. Taste again for seasoning.

*4* Spoon the pâté into individual pots. Garnish with flat leaf parsley and serve with thin slices of toast and sticks of cucumber, chicory and celery.

# Barley Soup

Eastern Europe has winters that are bitterly cold and traditional soups often contained beans, lentils and barley. In a climate with less fierce winters, a lighter soup with only one "filler" is more appealing, but the base of a good stock makes all the difference to the flavour.

## INGREDIENTS

*Serves 4*
900g/2lb meaty bones (lamb, beef or veal)
900ml/1½ pints/3¾ cups water
3 carrots
4 celery sticks
1 onion
30ml/2 tbsp oil
30ml/2 tbsp barley
salt and ground black pepper

—————— COOK'S TIP ——————

All soups taste better with home-made stock. The long slow simmering can be done well in advance and stocks freeze well. A quick (and more salty) version can be made using water and a stock cube, but it won't have the same flavour.

*1* Preheat the oven to 200°C/400°F/ Gas 6. To prepare the meat stock, brown the lamb, beef or veal bones in a roasting tin in the oven for about 30 minutes. Remove the bones and put them in a large saucepan, cover with water and bring to the boil.

*2* Use a metal spoon to skim off the froth which comes to the surface and then cover the pan and simmer for at least 2 hours. Chop the carrots, celery and onion finely. Heat the oil in a saucepan and sauté the vegetables in the oil for about 1 minute. Strain the stock into the pan.

*3* Add the barley to the pan of vegetables and continue cooking for about 1 hour, until the barley is soft. Season the soup with plenty of salt and pepper, transfer to serving bowls and serve hot.

# Chicken Soup with Lockshen

The best of all soup recipes, it is simple to make, if you follow two rules: make it the day before and try to find a boiling fowl which has much more flavour than a roasting bird.

### INGREDIENTS

*Serves 6–8*

3kg/6½lb boiling chicken, including the giblets, but not the liver
1 litre/1¾ pints/4 cups cold water
2 onions, halved
2 carrots
5 sticks celery
a handful of fine vermicelli (*lockshen*), about 115g/4oz
salt and ground black pepper
fresh bread, to serve (optional)

*1* Put the washed chicken into a very large pan with the giblets. Add the water and bring to the boil over high heat. Skim off the white froth that comes to the top and then add the halved onions, carrots and sticks of celery. Season with ground black pepper only.

*2* When the liquid comes to the boil again, turn the heat to low, cover and simmer the chicken and the stock for at least 2 hours. Keep an eye on the water level and add a little more so that the chicken is always covered.

*3* When the chicken is tender, take it out and take the meat off the bones, reserving it for another use. Put the bones back in the soup and continue cooking for a further 1 hour. There should be at least 1 litre/1¾ pints/4 cups of soup.

*4* Strain the soup into a large bowl and chill overnight. When it is quite cold it may form a jelly and a pale layer of fat will have settled on the top. Remove the fat with a spoon and discard.

*5* Bring the soup to the boil again, season to taste and add the vermicelli (*lockshen*). Boil for about 8 minutes and serve in large bowls, with fresh bread, if using.

# White Bean Soup

Use either haricot beans or butter beans for this velvety soup. As with all meat-based soups, real butter or cream is not included.

## INGREDIENTS

*Serves 4*

175g/6oz/³⁄₄ cup dried white beans or
    400g/14oz can cannellini or
    butter beans
2 large onions, chopped
4 celery sticks, chopped
1 parsnip, chopped
30–45ml/2–3 tbsp oil
1 litre/1³⁄₄ pints/4 cups meat stock
salt and ground black pepper
chopped fresh coriander and paprika,
    to garnish
fresh bread, to serve

1 If using dried beans, soak them overnight in cold water. Drain and boil rapidly in fresh water for 10 minutes, drain and simmer in fresh water until soft. Reserve the liquid and discard any bean skins on the surface.

2 Heat the oil and sauté the onions, celery and parsnip for 3 minutes.

3 Add the cooked beans (if using canned ones, drain them first and discard the liquid). Add the meat stock and continue cooking until the vegetables are tender. Allow the soup to cool slightly and using a food processor or hand blender, blend the soup until it is velvety smooth.

4 Reheat the soup gently, adding some of the bean liquid or some more water if it is too thick. Adjust the seasoning to taste.

5 To serve, transfer the soup into wide bowls. Serve with bread, garnish with coriander and sprinkle with a little paprika.

# Chicken Soup with Luft Knaidlach

During the Festival of Passover when no bread or pasta is eaten, chicken soup is served with light dumplings (*knaidlach*). There are two kinds, both of Ashkenazi (Eastern European) origin. The secret of making them light is to make both mixtures soft, and to chill the mixture before cooking.

## INGREDIENTS

*Makes enough for 12, allowing 3 small balls per person*
175g/6oz/¾ cup medium-ground
   matzo meal
150ml/¼ pint/⅔ cup cold water
5ml/1 tsp salt
pinch of ground ginger
3 eggs, well-beaten
90ml/6 tbsp oil
1 quantity Chicken Soup

*1* Mix the matzo meal with the water, salt and ginger. Add the eggs and oil and chill the mixture in the fridge for a few hours.

*2* Form the mixture into small balls about 2cm/¾in diameter, wetting your hands or dipping them in a little more meal as you work to prevent the mixture from sticking. Don't add too much meal or it will make the dumplings heavy.

*3* Bring a large pan of water to the boil and gently put in the *knaidlach*. As the water comes to the boil again, they will rise to the surface and double in size. Cook in gently boiling water for 20 minutes.

*4* Meanwhile reheat the Chicken Soup. Drain the *knaidlach*, pouring away the cooking water and float the dumplings in the soup. Transfer to soup bowls and serve.

# Chicken Soup with Matzo Kleis Balls

## INGREDIENTS

2 matzot (sheets of unleavened bread)
1 onion, chopped
30ml/2 tbsp oil
a handful of parsley
2 eggs
30–60ml/2–4 tbsp medium-ground
   matzo meal
pinch of ground ginger
1 quantity Chicken Soup
salt and ground black pepper

─── COOK'S TIP ───

You can make both types of dumpling well in advance, but the balls should be kept chilled. They also freeze well, so it is a good idea to cook half and freeze half. To cook from frozen, leave them to defrost for about 1 hour and then cook them in soup.

*1* Soak the matzot in cold water for about 5 minutes and then drain and squeeze them dry.

*2* Fry the onion in the oil until golden. Chop the parsley, reserving a few sprigs for the garnish. Whisk the eggs slightly.

*3* Mix together the soaked matzot, fried onion, parsley and eggs. Season with salt, pepper and ginger and add about 15ml/1 tbsp of matzo meal. Chill for at least 1 hour.

*4* Roll the mixture into small balls, drop them into the fast-boiling soup and cook for about 20 minutes. Serve, garnished with the parsley.

# Jerusalem Artichoke Soup

### INGREDIENTS

*Serves 4*

30−60ml/2−4 tbsp butter
115g/4oz/2 cups sliced mushrooms
2 onions, chopped
450g/1lb Jerusalem artichokes, peeled
 and sliced
300ml/½ pint/1¼ cups vegetable stock
300ml/½ pint/1¼ cups milk
salt and ground black pepper

---
— COOK'S TIP —

To make a light vegetable stock, simply boil some carrots, onion, leek or root vegetables in a large pan of water. Simmer for about 30 minutes and then strain.

---

*1* Melt the butter in a saucepan and sauté the mushrooms for 1 minute. Put them on a plate and then sauté the onions and artichokes, adding a little more butter if necessary. Keep on stirring the vegetables without allowing them to brown.

*2* Add the vegetable stock to the pan and bring to the boil. Simmer until the artichokes are soft and then season to taste.

*3* Purée the soup with a hand blender or food processor, adding the milk slowly until smooth. Reheat the soup, return the mushrooms to the pan and serve.

# Tomato and Red Pepper Soup

A late summer soup using very ripe peppers and tomatoes. It can be served cold but won't be nearly as tasty if made with imported winter vegetables which have a less vibrant flavour.

### INGREDIENTS

*Serves 4*

5 large tomatoes
30−60ml/2−4 tbsp olive oil
1 onion, chopped
450g/1lb thinly sliced red or
 orange peppers
30ml/2 tbsp tomato purée
a pinch of sugar
475ml/16fl oz/2 cups vegetable stock
60ml/4 tbsp soured cream (optional)
salt and ground black pepper
chopped fresh dill, to garnish

*1* Skin the tomatoes by plunging them into boiling water for 30 seconds. Chop the flesh and reserve any juice.

*2* Heat half the oil in a saucepan and sauté the onion over moderate heat until soft. Add the peppers and the remaining oil and continue cooking, without browning the vegetables, until they start to soften.

*3* Stir in the chopped tomatoes, tomato purée, the seasoning, sugar and a few tablespoons of stock and simmer until the vegetables are tender.

*4* Stir in the rest of the stock and blend until smooth. Strain to remove the skins, and season.

*5* Pour into bowls, swirl in the cream, if using, and garnish with dill.

# FISH AND VEGETARIAN DISHES

*Concern about animal welfare means that many people prefer not to eat meat, so fish is very popular. Although smoked salmon is a must for special occasions like weddings and barmitzvahs, it's just as usual to serve both herring and fried gefilte fish which are cheap.*

*When entertaining friends it is often easier to choose a dinner based on vegetables and fish. I've included some old favourites as well as several new inventions. The vegetarian cholent for Saturday lunch is a warming winter dish which would be equally good for busy working cooks as it simmers all day and needs no attention.*

# Halibut in Lemon Sauce

## INGREDIENTS

*Serves 4*

1 small onion
1 large carrot
300ml/½ pint/1¼ cups water
2.5ml/½ tsp sugar
4 halibut steaks, about 175g/6oz each
2 lemons
3 egg yolks
salt and ground black pepper
asparagus and boiled potatoes, to serve

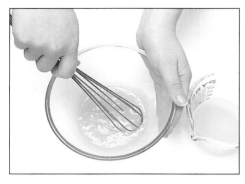

*1* Slice the onion and carrot and bring to the boil with the water in a wide pan. Season with sugar, salt and pepper and simmer for 15 minutes. Remove the vegetable pieces with a slotted spoon and put aside. Lower the halibut steaks into the cooking liquid and cook over low heat for about 8 minutes.

*2* You can tell when the halibut steaks are cooked by inserting a knife near the bone, if the fish looks opaque it is cooked. Lift the steaks out and arrange them on a shallow dish. Cover with a sheet of foil if you want to serve them hot. Bring the cooking liquid to the boil again and reduce it over high heat for a few minutes.

*3* Meanwhile, to make the lemon sauce, cut a few slices from the top of each lemon and set them aside for garnishing. Squeeze the juice from the remaining pieces of lemon, whisk the egg yolks in a bowl and stir in the lemon juice.

*4* Strain the reduced cooking liquid on to the egg and lemon mixture and pour it back into the pan. Stir the sauce over very low heat, taking great care not to let it boil. When it thickens, pour it over the fish. Serve the fish hot or cold, with asparagus and boiled potatoes.

# *Whole Cooked Salmon*

Farmed salmon has made this fish more affordable and less of a treat but a whole salmon still features as a centrepiece at parties. It is never served with cold meats but is accompanied by salads and mayonnaise. As with all fish, the taste depends first on freshness and second on not overcooking it, so although you need to start early, the cooking time is short.

## INGREDIENTS

*Serves about 10 as part of a buffet*
2–3kg/5–6lb fresh whole salmon
30ml/2 tbsp oil
1 lemon
salt and ground black pepper
lemon wedges, cucumber and fresh dill
    sprigs, to garnish

*1* Preheat the oven to 200°C/400°F/ Gas 6. Wash the salmon and dry it well, inside and out. Pour half the oil on to a large piece of strong foil and place the fish in the centre.

*2* Put a few slices of lemon inside the salmon and arrange some more on the top. Season well and sprinkle over the remaining oil. Wrap up the foil to make a loose parcel. Put the parcel on another sheet of foil or a baking sheet and cook in the oven for 10 minutes. Turn off the oven, don't open the door and leave for several hours. As it cools the salmon cooks but stays moist.

*3* To serve the same day, remove the foil and peel off the skin. If you are keeping it for the following day, leave the skin on and chill the fish overnight. Arrange the fish on a large platter and garnish with lemon wedges, cucumber cut into thin ribbons and sprigs of dill.

# Smoked Salmon Parcels

Smoked salmon is a favourite filling for snacks and sandwiches.

### INGREDIENTS

*Makes about 20 small appetizers*
350g/12oz best quality smoked salmon
2 lemons
bunch of fresh dill, to garnish

### Fish filling
225g/8oz smoked mackerel fillet
45ml/3 tbsp smatana or crème fraîche
ground black pepper

### Cheese and herb filling
bunch of mixed herbs, such as chives,
   parsley and chervil
225g/8oz curd or ricotta cheese
salt and ground black pepper

*1* To make the fish filling, remove the skin from the mackerel and make sure there are no bones. Blend or mash the fish with the smatana or crème fraîche. Add pepper but no salt as both the salmon and mackerel are quite salty. To make the cheese filling simply chop the herbs and stir them into the soft cheese and season well.

*2* Cut the smoked salmon into strips about 2.5 x 7.5cm/1 x 3in. Put a teaspoon of the chosen filling at one end and roll up, smoothing the sides with a knife to make sure the filling is neatly enclosed.

*3* Arrange the rolls on a platter and garnish with lemon and dill.

# Cucumber and Fish Salad

A cool dish for summer – ideal served on individual plates for lunch or on a large platter as part of a buffet. Instead of cod you can use haddock fillet, or for a more special occasion, sea bass.

### INGREDIENTS

*Serves 4–8*
2 large cucumbers
500g/1¼lb fresh cod fillet, skinned
1 spring onion, chopped
small bunch of fresh dill
75ml/5 tbsp milk
60ml/4 tbsp mayonnaise
30ml/2 tbsp crème fraîche or
   natural yogurt
175g/6oz/¾ cup cooked broad beans
   or peas (optional)
4 black or green olives and cucumber
   ribbons, to garnish
salt

*1* Skin one of the cucumbers and cut the flesh into dice. With a vegetable peeler, remove about six long thin strips from the other cucumber and then cut the rest into dice as well. Sprinkle the pieces with salt and leave to drain on absorbent kitchen paper.

*2* Put the fish in a pan with the spring onion, a few sprigs of dill and the milk. Season well and poach gently for a few minutes until the fish begins to flake. Lift it out with a slotted spoon and leave to cool.

*3* Wash and drain the cucumber cubes and dry well. Mix the mayonnaise with the crème fraîche or yogurt, stir in the cucumber, broad beans or peas, if using, and finally fold in the fish.

*4* Spoon the mixture on to plates, and garnish with olives and cucumber ribbons.

# Gefilte Fish

There are two ways of cooking this popular snack, either by poaching or frying.

## INGREDIENTS

*Makes about 24 small balls*

900g/2lb mixed filleted fish, such as
   carp, bream, haddock and cod
1 large onion
2 eggs
5–10ml/1–2 tsp sugar
50g/2oz/10 tbsp medium-ground
   matzo meal
salt and ground black pepper
oil, for frying
flat leaf parsley, to garnish
bottled beetroot and horseradish sauce,
   to serve

*1* Cut the fish and the onion into small pieces and process briefly together in a food processor. Add the eggs, sugar, salt and pepper and continue to blend until the mixture is smooth. Taste the mixture (raw fresh fish is not unpleasant) and add more seasoning if necessary.

*2* Stir in a few spoonfuls of matzo meal and form the mixture into 2.5cm/1in balls. The mixture will seem quite soft.

*3* Roll the balls in the remaining matzo meal and chill until you are ready to fry them. Heat a large pan of oil until it reaches a temperature of 190°C/375°F. Fry the balls for about 4–5 minutes until they are crisp and golden brown.

*4* Lift them out with a slotted spoon and drain very well. Cool.

*5* Serve cold, with beetroot and horseradish sauce, garnished with flat leaf parsley.

# *Fried Fish*

Fried fish is nearly always served cold. If you have never tried it, you are missing a real speciality. A tray of different fish is usual, but you can use one variety if you prefer. The usual accompaniment is potato salad and pickled cucumbers.

### INGREDIENTS

*Serves 8*

2 Dover sole, about 225g/8oz each
2 large plaice, about 450g/1lb each
1 thick cod fillet, about 450g/
    1lb, skinned
1.5 litres/2½ pints/6¼ cups oil,
    for frying
45ml/3 tbsp flour
40–50g/1½–2oz/8–10 tbsp medium-
    ground matzo meal
4 eggs
salt and ground black pepper
lemon wedges, to garnish
potato salad and pickled cucumbers,
    to serve

*1* Wash and dry the fish very well. Leave the Dover sole whole, but cut the plaice across the main bone in the centre into three sections. Cut the cod fillet into two or three pieces. Start heating the oil in a large deep pan. It will take 4–6 minutes for 2.5cm/1in of oil to reach a hot enough temperature (190°C/375°F). If you have not got a thermometer, then drop a cube of bread into the oil and it should brown in 30 seconds.

*2* Put the flour and the matzo meal on separate plates and the eggs in a glass dish. Season the eggs and the matzo meal.

*3* Dip each piece of fish first into the flour and then into the beaten egg. Lift it out immediately and dip it into the matzo meal.

*4* Lower the fish into the hot oil. Don't put in too many pieces as this reduces the temperature of the oil. Fry for about 6 minutes. Turn the fish over and when it is crisp and brown, lift it out with a slotted spoon. Drain over the oil and cool on kitchen paper. Serve with potato salad and pickled cucumbers, garnished with lemon.

# Stuffed Vegetables

Cabbage or grape leaves are often used for stuffing. You can use any vegetable, such as onions or tomatoes. Peppers and courgettes are also good eaten cold.

## INGREDIENTS

*Serves 6–8*
2 small red and 2 small yellow peppers
4 courgettes
30–60ml/2–4 tbsp olive oil
225g/8oz/1 cup basmati rice
2 dried peaches or apricots
1.5ml/¼ tsp tomato purée
pinch of ground cinnamon
1.5ml/¼ tsp paprika
small bunch of flat leaf parsley
salt and ground black pepper

*1* Preheat the oven to 190°C/375°F/ Gas 5. Cut the tops off the peppers and remove the seeds and membranes.

*2* Cut the ends off the courgettes and remove the centres with a corer.

*3* Heat half the oil in a roasting tin for 5 minutes. Put in the vegetables and roast for about 20 minutes. Drizzle the remaining oil over the top.

*4* Meanwhile cook the rice. Bring a large pan of water to the boil, add the rice and boil for about 8 minutes or until tender, but not mushy. Drain.

*5* Snip the dried peaches or apricots into slivers with kitchen scissors, and stir into the rice with the tomato purée, spices and seasoning. Chop some of the parsley and mix about 45ml/3 tbsp into the rice. Pour a little oil from the vegetables into the rice.

*6* Cool the vegetables slightly and stuff with the rice. Put the tops on the peppers and arrange the vegetables on a serving dish. Garnish with parsley.

# Vegetarian Cholent

The slow-cooked meal for Sabbath lunch is called cholent. It is usually a meat dish but here is a vegetarian version. The intense flavour comes from slow simmering of the vegetables.

## INGREDIENTS

*Serves 6*
6 onions
3 carrots
4 potatoes
6 sticks celery
45–75ml/3–5 tbsp oil
275g/10oz dark, flat mushrooms
15ml/1 tbsp paprika
60ml/4 tbsp soy sauce
90g/3½oz/½ cup barley
475ml/16fl oz/2 cups boiling water
salt and ground black pepper

*1* Cut the onions into quarters and the carrots and potatoes into 2cm/¾in dice. Cut the celery into 2.5cm/1in pieces.

*2* Heat half of the oil in a large frying pan and sauté the onions until they begin to turn brown. Add the carrots and continue cooking for about 1 minute. Transfer the onions, carrots and celery to the slow-cooker.

*3* Sauté the mushrooms in the remaining oil and add them to the cooker. Sprinkle the paprika over the oil and cook briefly. Add the soy sauce, the barley and the boiling water and stir.

*4* Put the potatoes in the pot with the liquid, season well and cover. Cook on the lowest heat for at least 6 hours or, for the authentic version, leave to cook overnight.

# Aubergines with Cheese

Cheese is never served as a separate course after meat. However it often features as part of a fish or vegetarian buffet.

## INGREDIENTS

*Serves 4*
2 large aubergines
450g/1lb tomatoes
1 onion
75–105ml/5–7 tbsp olive oil
175g/6oz kosher Dutch or Cheddar cheese, thinly sliced
salt and ground black pepper
green salad, to serve

*1* Cut the aubergines crossways into 1cm/½in slices. Sprinkle them with salt and leave to drain on absorbent kitchen paper for 30 minutes. Rinse well and then dry. Skin and slice the tomatoes.

*2* Chop the onion finely and sauté it in a few tablespoons of olive oil until golden. Set aside on a plate. Heat the remaining oil and fry the aubergine slices on both sides until brown. Season the vegetables lightly.

*3* Preheat the oven to 190°C/375°F/ Gas 5. Put a layer of aubergine slices into an oiled casserole. Sprinkle over some of the onion and then add some tomato slices. Cover with slices of cheese and continue making layers until all the ingredients are used up, finishing with a layer of cheese.

*4* Bake for 30–40 minutes until the cheese is bubbling and brown. Serve with green salad.

# *Matzo Pancakes*

Passover pancakes are made with matzo meal instead of flour. They can have a savoury topping or can simply be served with a liberal sprinkling of sugar and ground cinnamon.

## INGREDIENTS

*Serves 2 – makes 10 x 6cm/2¹/₂in pancakes*
**For the pancakes**
1 egg white
1 whole egg
120ml/4fl oz/¹/₂ cup water
pinch of salt
40g/1¹/₂ oz fine-ground matzo meal
30−45ml/2−3 tbsp oil

**For the savoury topping**
225g/8oz fresh spinach
50g/2oz Cheddar cheese, grated
salt and ground black pepper

*1* To make the topping: wash the spinach very well, drain and cook in a pan with no extra water for about 1 minute. Put it in a sieve, press out the moisture and then chop it. Season well. Stir in half the cheese.

*2* For the pancakes, whisk the egg white and the whole egg until thick and then gradually add the water and salt. Sprinkle in the matzo meal and beat until the mixture is smooth.

*3* Heat a little of the oil in a small frying pan and when it is hot, drop some of the mixture in large spoonfuls into the oil. Almost immediately turn them over and press the pancakes down slightly. Cook for another minute on the other side.

*4* Repeat until the mixture is used up. While you are cooking the pancakes, heat the grill. Arrange the pancakes on a baking tray. Cover each one with a little of the spinach mixture and grate the remaining cheese over the top. Grill for 1−2 minutes to melt the cheese and serve immediately.

# MEAT

*Grilled or roasted meat is often served during the week rather than at weekends, and although veal and venison could be on the menu, it is more likely to be lamb or beef. A large joint of brisket is used for the famous salt beef, and this is one of the best dishes to order in a restaurant. Kebabs of lamb and spicy sausages are barbecued. Perhaps the most traditional Jewish food is the overnight Sabbath "cholent". The word probably comes from the French* chaud-lent *meaning warm and slow, as the meat is first browned and surrounded with filling vegetables, then cooked slowly overnight. Originally everyone took their pot to the local village bakery but nowadays a slow-cooker is the answer.*

# Steak Salad

In most countries kosher beef comes from the forequarter, so it lacks the tenderness of fillet and rump. Rare-cooked steak with vegetables makes a well-flavoured main course salad.

**INGREDIENTS**

*Serves 4*
500g/1¼lb new potatoes
115g/4oz young carrots
1 sprig of mint
225g/8oz French beans
450g/1lb rare-grilled steak or cooked roast beef
150ml/¼ pint/⅔ cup mayonnaise
salt and ground black pepper
lettuce leaves, 1 sliced yellow pepper and 6 black olives, to garnish

*1* Cook the potatoes and carrots separately in boiling salted water with a few mint leaves. When they are tender, pour them into a colander to drain. Cook the French beans for a few minutes in boiling salted water or until they are just tender. Drain and leave the beans to cool.

*2* Cut the rare-grilled steak or cooked roast beef into small dice. Mix the vegetables with the mayonnaise and fold in the meat. Season to taste.

*3* Pile the steak salad into the centre of a large dish and garnish with lettuce leaves, sliced yellow pepper and black olives.

---

# Veal Schnitzels with Lemon

In Israel where meat is expensive they have perfected the art of turkey farming. Thin slices of turkey breast can be used instead of the original Austrian veal schnitzels or "slivers".

**INGREDIENTS**

*Serves 4*
675g/1½lb thin slices of veal or turkey
30ml/2 tbsp flour
3 eggs
225g/8oz/1 cup medium-ground matzo meal
oil, for frying
salt and ground black pepper
2 lemons, cut into wedges, to garnish
lettuce leaves, to serve

*1* Pound the meat with a tenderizing mallet until the slices are very thin. Toss the meat slices in the flour, seasoned with salt and pepper.

*2* Beat the eggs in a shallow dish and put the matzo meal on a large plate. Dip the floured veal or turkey first into the beaten eggs then into the matzo meal, until well coated.

*3* Heat about 1cm/½in oil in a large frying pan and when it is very hot (test with a cube of bread) lower in some of the schnitzels in a single layer. Cook for about 5 minutes and then turn the slices over. Cook the other side for 5 minutes or until golden.

*4* Arrange the cooked schnitzels on a serving dish and keep them warm in a low oven until you have finished frying them all. Garnish with wedges of lemon and serve with lettuce leaves.

# Peppers Stuffed with Minced Beef

A lunch or buffet dish which makes a change from rice or wheat-stuffed vegetables.

## INGREDIENTS

*Serves 4*
4 red peppers
1 onion
2 sticks celery
450g/1lb minced lean beef
60ml/4 tbsp olive oil
50g/2oz button mushrooms
pinch of ground cinnamon
salt and ground black pepper
chervil or flat leaf parsley, to garnish
green salad, to serve

*1* Cut the tops off the red peppers and reserve them. Remove the seeds and membranes from the peppers. Finely chop the onion and the sticks of celery. Set aside.

*2* Sauté the minced beef in a non-stick frying pan for a few minutes, stirring until it is no longer red. Transfer to a plate. Pour half the oil into the frying pan and sauté the chopped vegetables over high heat until the onion starts to brown. Add the mushrooms and stir in the partly cooked beef. Season with the cinnamon, salt and pepper. Cook over low heat for about 30 minutes.

*3* Preheat the oven to 190°C/375°F/ Gas 5. Cut a sliver off the base of each pepper to make sure they stand level, spoon in the beef and vegetable mixture and replace the lids. Arrange in an oiled baking dish, drizzle over the remaining oil and cook in the oven for 30 minutes. Serve with green salad.

---
COOK'S TIP

Instead of peppers you can use large onions or tomatoes. Parboil the onions for about 10 minutes and remove the centres. Carefully scoop out the seeds and flesh of the tomatoes. Fill with the minced beef mixture and bake as above.

# Beef Cholent with Beans and Hamin Eggs

There are many different versions of this slow-cooked casserole. This one has the addition of Sephardi whole eggs which are cooked to a soft texture and are honey-coloured.

## INGREDIENTS

*Serves 6–8*
225g/8oz/1¼ cups haricot or butter beans
6 small eggs
10 small onions
2 carrots
30–60ml/2–4 tbsp oil
1.5kg/3–3½lb stewing steak, cubed
5ml/1tsp paprika
5ml/1tsp tomato purée
600ml/1 pint/2½ cups boiling water or beef stock
salt and ground black pepper

1 Soak the beans in cold water overnight. Drain and bring to the boil in fresh water. Cook rapidly for 10 minutes, skimming off the white froth and any bean skins that come to the surface. Drain and reserve the cooking liquid for another use. Hard boil the eggs for 10 minutes.

2 Preheat a slow-cooker to Auto. Halve the onions and dice the carrots. Heat half the oil in a pan and sauté the onions until brown, then transfer to the slow-cooker with the carrots and beans. Brown the beef in the remaining oil and place on top of the vegetables. Arrange the eggs in between pieces of meat.

3 Stir the paprika, tomato purée and seasoning into the oil left in the pan and cook for 1 minute. Add the boiling water or stock to deglaze the pan and pour over the meat and eggs.

4 Cover the pot and leave the cholent to cook for at least 8 hours or as long as 20 hours. Take out the eggs, remove the shells and return them to the casserole before serving.

— COOK'S TIP —

For overnight cooking, a slow cooker is the best method since the liquid does not evaporate. In a conventional oven, cook the cholent overnight, at 110°C/225°F/Gas ¼, but add enough water or stock to almost fill the pot.

# Lamb with Lentils and Apricots

## INGREDIENTS

*Serves 4–6*
2 large onions
2 large carrots
30–60ml/2–4 tbsp oil
900g/2lb lean lamb
5cm/2in stick cinnamon or
   2.5ml/½ tsp ground cinnamon
1.5ml/¼ tsp ground turmeric
1.5ml/¼ tsp chilli powder
225g/8oz/1 cup green lentils
1 litre/1¾ pints/4 cups water
12 ready-to-eat dried apricots
chopped fresh parsley, to garnish

*1* Preheat the oven to 180°C/350°F/ Gas 4. Cut the onions and carrots into large chunks. Heat half the oil in a flameproof casserole and sauté the vegetables until the onion starts to brown. Put the vegetables on a plate and set aside.

*2* Cut the lamb into 2.5cm/1in cubes and sauté over medium heat, adding more oil if necessary to brown them all over. Add the cinnamon stick or ground cinnamon and sprinkle the rest of the spices over the lamb.

*3* Rinse the lentils and add them to the casserole with the vegetables. Stir in 750ml/1¼ pints/3 cups boiling water, season and bring to the boil. Cover and transfer to the oven.

*4* Cook for 1 hour and check to see that the lentils haven't absorbed all the liquid, adding the remaining water if necessary. Cook for a further hour.

*5* Add the apricots and press them down under the gravy, turn off the oven and leave them to swell for about 20 minutes. Remove the cinnamon stick if using, check the seasoning and stir in a little more water if it seems too dry. Garnish with chopped parsley.

---

# Braised Beef with Vegetables

On Friday evenings in the winter Sabbath begins early, at dusk. A rich-tasting braised beef casserole is ideal as it can be started in the afternoon and left to cook slowly. By dinner time it will be tender and piping hot.

## INGREDIENTS

*Serves 6–8*
30–45ml/2–3 tbsp oil
1.5kg/3½lb rolled brisket or beef
   top rib
8 small onions
2 large carrots
1 head celery
475ml/16fl oz/2 cups beef stock
salt and ground black pepper
sprig of flat leaf parsley, to garnish

*1* Preheat the oven to 180°C/350°F/ Gas 4. Heat the oil in a casserole and brown the beef all over. Add the onions and brown them. Cut the carrots and celery into large pieces and add them to the pan. Cook for a further 2–3 minutes.

*2* Meanwhile, add 450ml/¾ pint/ 1⅞ cups hot stock to the beef. Bring to the boil, season and cover.

*3* Cook in the oven for about 2 hours. Turn the joint over and add more stock if necessary. There should be enough liquid to come half way up the meat and to make a thin, but rich gravy. Continue cooking for about 1 hour.

*4* Slice the meat and serve, surrounded by the vegetables. Garnish with flat leaf parsley.

# Roasted Lamb with Courgettes

Racks of tender, baby lamb chops, roasted pink on the inside, are a favourite choice for wedding dinners.

### INGREDIENTS

*Serves 4*

2 small racks lamb, each with 6 chops
60ml/4 tbsp olive oil
juice of 1 pomegranate
15ml/1 tbsp French mustard
4 sprigs fresh mint
4 courgettes, quartered lengthways
120ml/4fl oz/½ cup light vegetable or
    chicken stock
30ml/2 tbsp toasted pine nuts
salt and ground black pepper

*1* Arrange the racks of lamb in a glass or ceramic dish. In a glass jug mix together 15ml/1 tbsp olive oil, the pomegranate juice, mustard, salt and pepper. Add a few mint leaves and pour this marinade over the lamb. Chill for a couple of hours.

*2* Preheat the oven to 230°C/450°F/ Gas 8. Pour the remaining oil into a dish and put in the oven to heat. Add the courgettes to the hot oil, turning them to coat both sides.

*3* Put the lamb in a roasting tin, with the fat side up. Roast the lamb and the courgettes for 20 minutes.

*4* Transfer the racks of lamb to a serving dish and let them rest for 5 minutes, lightly covered with a sheet of foil. Pour the remaining marinade into the roasting tin and deglaze the pan with the vegetable or chicken stock. Heat and pour into a sauce boat.

*5* Slice each rack of lamb into chops and arrange them on plates. Sprinkle the pine nuts over the courgettes. Serve the sauce separately and garnish the lamb with mint.

---

COOK'S TIP

To make pomegranate juice, halve the fruit and squeeze, like a lemon.

# Slow-cooked Lamb with Barley

A perfect Sabbath dish which can be cooked for many hours.

## INGREDIENTS

*Serves 4–6*

15–30ml/1–2 tbsp oil
900g/2lb shoulder of lamb, cubed
2 large onions
6 carrots or potatoes
115g/4oz/²⁄₃ cup barley
750ml–1.2 litres/1¼–2 pints/3–5
   cups boiling stock or water and
   1 kosher beef stock cube
chopped thyme, to garnish
salt and ground black pepper

*1* Heat half the oil in a non-stick frying pan and sauté the cubes of lamb until brown all over. Transfer the meat to a large plate.

*2* Cut the onions and carrots into small pieces (thinly slice the potatoes, if using) and sauté these in the remaining oil. Add the barley and seasoning, pour in half the stock and bring the liquid to the boil. Cook for about 5 minutes.

*3* Pour the vegetables and barley into the base of a slow-cooker, cover with the lamb cubes and add enough stock to make a gravy. (See Cook's Tip). Cover and cook for 6–9 hours or more. Check for seasoning, stir well and serve garnished with thyme.

—— COOK'S TIP ——

A slow-cooker is ideal for very gentle cooking as the gravy will not dry up. If you are using a conventional low oven, at 110°C/225°F/Gas ¼, the liquid tends to evaporate, so it's a good idea to add a little more than you would expect.

# VEGETABLES AND SIDE DISHES

*Vegetables are never simply boiled or steamed;*
*they are fried or roasted to accentuate their taste.*
*Onions are essential for the sweet flavour they give*
*to almost any meat dish. Stuffed or grilled*
*peppers, aubergines and courgettes are popular in*
*Sephardi cooking, as is garlic.*
*As well as salads of mixed green leaves there are*
*rice salads with nuts and dried fruits, and cracked*
*wheat, which is transformed into tabbouleh with*
*fresh mint and parsley. Potato salad is a must.*
*Fresh, young vegetables like beetroot and green*
*cucumbers make any table look attractive, but the*
*original idea for large families was to stretch the*
*main course with filling side dishes.*

# Roasted Pepper Salad

Peppers in mixed packs include green ones, but the orange, yellow and red are the sweetest. This colourful salad can be served either as a starter or as an attractive side dish to accompany cold meat dishes.

### INGREDIENTS

*Serves 6–10 as part of a buffet*
6 peppers, in mixed colours
90–120ml/6–8 tbsp olive oil
salt and ground black pepper

*1* Preheat the oven to 190°C/375°F/ Gas 5. Halve the peppers and remove all the seeds and membranes. Cut them into 2.5cm/1in strips.

*2* Pour half of the oil into a roasting tin and put the tin into the oven for a few minutes to heat. Arrange the peppers in a single layer over the oil, turning them to make sure they are well-coated. Season well and drizzle over the remaining oil.

*3* Roast for 20–30 minutes, turning them around once to see that those at the edges don't brown more than those in the centre.

*4* Turn the peppers out on to a large plate and leave to cool slightly. With a sharp knife peel off the charred skin. Arrange the peeled peppers in groups of red, yellow and green on a decorative dish.

---

# Tabbouleh

A salad that actually improves if it is made the day before. The bulgur or cracked wheat is uncooked and absorbs the moisture and flavour of the vegetables and dressing.

### INGREDIENTS

*Serves 4–6*
225g/8oz/1 cup bulgur wheat
15cm/6in piece of cucumber
2 tomatoes
3–4 spring onions
several sprigs of fresh mint (about 60ml/4 tbsp chopped)
about 90ml/6 tbsp finely chopped fresh parsley
75ml/5 tbsp olive oil
30ml/2 tbsp lemon juice
salt and ground black pepper

*1* Cover the bulgur wheat with water and leave to soak in a bowl for about 30 minutes. Drain it through a fine sieve.

*2* Peel and dice the cucumber. Skin the tomatoes by soaking for a minute in boiling water. Chop the flesh into small pieces, discarding the seeds. Slice the spring onions.

*3* Mix the drained wheat with the vegetables and herbs. Whisk the oil with the lemon juice and seasoning and stir into the wheat. Chill until required but serve at room temperature.

> ——— COOK'S TIP ———
>
> Tabbouleh can either be served with pitta bread or eaten in the fingers, wrapped in lettuce leaves.

# Pickled Cucumbers

Often served with salt beef, these gherkins or cucumbers are simple to prepare but take a couple of days for the flavour to develop.

## INGREDIENTS

*Serves 6–8*
6 small pickling cucumbers
75ml/5 tbsp white wine vinegar
475ml/16fl oz/2 cups cold water
15ml/1 tbsp salt
10ml/2 tsp sugar
10 black peppercorns
1 garlic clove
1 bunch fresh dill (optional)

*1* You will need a large lidded jar or an oblong non-metallic container with a tightly fitting lid. Cut each cucumber lengthways into six spears.

*2* Mix together the wine vinegar, water, salt and sugar. Crush a few of the peppercorns and leave the rest whole. Add them to the liquid. Cut the garlic clove in half.

*3* Arrange the cucumber spears in the jar or container, pour over the pickling liquid and add the garlic. Put in a few sprigs of dill if using. Make sure they are completely submerged.

*4* Leave the cucumbers, covered, in the fridge for at least two days. To serve, lift them out and discard the garlic, dill and peppercorns. Store any uneaten cucumbers in their pickling liquid in the fridge.

# Potato Salads

Most people adore potato salad made with a creamy mayonnaise. These two versions are lighter and more summery. The first should be served warm – the second can be prepared a day ahead and served cold.

## INGREDIENTS

*Serves 4*
900g/2 lb new potatoes
5ml/1 tsp salt

**Dressing for warm salad**
30ml/2 tbsp hazelnut or walnut oil
60ml/4 tbsp sunflower oil
juice of 1 lemon
15 pistachio nuts
salt and ground black pepper
flat leaf parsley, to garnish

**Dressing for cold salad**
1 bunch parsley (about 90ml/
    6 tbsp, chopped)
2 large spring onions
75ml/5 tbsp olive oil
10ml/2 tsp white wine vinegar
1 garlic clove, crushed
salt and ground black pepper

*1* Scrub the new potatoes, cover with cold water and bring to the boil. Add the salt and cook for about 10–15 minutes until tender. Drain well and set aside.

*2* For the warm salad, mix together the hazelnut or walnut oil with the sunflower oil and lemon juice and season well.

*3* Use a knife to crush the pistachio nuts roughly.

*4* When the potatoes have cooled slightly, pour over the dressing and sprinkle with the chopped nuts. Serve garnished with flat leaf parsley.

*5* For the cold salad, cook the potatoes as above, drain and leave to cool. Meanwhile chop the parsley and the spring onions finely.

*6* Whisk together the oil, vinegar, garlic, seasoning and herbs and pour over the potatoes. Cover tightly and chill overnight. Allow to come to room temperature before serving.

# Spiced Rice

Rice is served for everyday meals and feasts. Tender baby lamb was used in a celebrated dish called 'King's Rice' but spices, nuts and dried fruit can be used to make boiled rice into a special dish.

### INGREDIENTS

*Serves 4–6*
225g/8oz/1 cup basmati rice
30ml/2 tbsp oil
2.5cm/1in cinnamon stick
1.5ml/¼ tsp ground turmeric
1.5ml/¼ tsp tomato purée
15ml/1 tbsp raisins
25g/1oz toasted almonds, to serve
salt and ground black pepper

*1* First make simple boiled rice. Using a sieve, rinse the rice in cold running water until the water runs clear.

*2* Add the rice to a saucepan of fast boiling water, add 5ml/1 tsp salt and boil for about 5–7 minutes or until the grains are tender. Drain and rinse with a little boiling water.

*3* To make fried rice, heat the oil in a large frying pan. Add the cinnamon stick and the turmeric and then the boiled rice. Stir well and heat thoroughly. Mix in the tomato purée and the raisins and taste for seasoning.

*4* Remove the cinnamon stick and serve, sprinkled with almonds.

---
COOK'S TIP
---

Pouring water through the boiled rice removes the starch. To make the fried rice you can boil the rice in advance and pour cold water through it and leave it to cool. Continue from Step 2, making sure the rice is quite hot before serving.

# Bulgur Pilaff

Bulgur – or cracked wheat – is far easier to cook than rice. For every cup of grain you simply need two cups of liquid. Then you can add herbs, nuts or dried fruits to make the pilaff more interesting.

### INGREDIENTS

*Serves 8*
2 onions
60ml/4 tbsp oil
450g/1lb/2 cups bulgur wheat
1 litre/1¾ pints/4 cups hot chicken or "chicken flavour" stock
2–3 sprigs fresh mint or flat leaf parsley
3–4 ready-to-eat dried apricots, sliced
45ml/3 tbsp pine nuts, toasted
salt and ground black pepper
sprig of mint, to garnish

*1* Chop the onions finely. Heat the oil in a large frying pan and when it is hot toss in the onion. Stir over medium to high heat until the onion is slightly browned.

*2* Wash the bulgur wheat and drain. Add the bulgur wheat to the sautéed onion and stir for a few minutes to coat the grains with the oil, adding a little more oil if necessary.

*3* Add the stock. Bring to the boil, turn off the heat and cover.

*4* Stand for 10 minutes. Meanwhile, chop the herbs. Check the seasoning and add the apricots.

*5* To serve, spoon the hot bulgur wheat into a large dish and sprinkle over the herbs and toasted pine nuts. Garnish with a sprig of mint.

# Spicy Carrots

Adding spices to the carrots before leaving them to cool infuses them with flavour – an ideal dish to serve cold the next day (or up to a week later, if you keep them in the fridge).

## INGREDIENTS

*Serves 4*
450g/1lb carrots
475ml/16fl oz/2 cups water
2.5ml/½ tsp salt
5ml/1 tsp cumin seeds
½–1 red chilli (to taste)
1 large garlic clove, crushed
30ml/2 tbsp olive oil
5ml/1 tsp paprika
juice of 1 lemon
flat leaf parsley, to garnish

*1* Cut the carrots into slices about 5mm/¼in thick. Bring the water to the boil and add the salt and carrot slices. Simmer for about 8 minutes or until the carrots are just tender, without allowing them to get too soft. Drain the carrots, put them into a bowl and set aside.

*2* Grind or crush the cumin to a powder. Remove the seeds from the chilli and chop the chilli finely. Take care when handling as they can irritate the skin and eyes.

*3* Gently heat the oil in a pan and toss in the garlic and the chilli. Stir over medium heat for about a minute, without allowing the garlic to brown. Stir in the paprika and the lemon juice.

*4* Pour the warm mixture over the carrots, tossing them well so they are coated with the spices. Spoon into a serving dish and garnish with a sprig of flat leaf parsley.

# Potato Latkes

*Latkes*, or pancakes, should be piping hot and are sometimes served with hot salt beef or salami. Or, serve as a delicious snack with apple sauce and soured cream.

## INGREDIENTS

*Serves 4*
2 medium potatoes
1 onion
1 size 1 egg, beaten
30ml/2 tbsp medium-ground
   matzo meal
oil, for frying
salt and ground black pepper

*1* Grate the potatoes and the onion coarsely. Put them in a large colander but don't rinse them. Press them down, squeezing out the thick starchy liquid.

*2* Immediately stir the beaten egg into the drained potato and onion mixture. Add the matzo meal, stirring well to mix. Season with plenty of pepper and salt.

*3* Pour some oil into a frying pan to a depth of about 1cm/½in. Heat the oil for a few minutes (test it by throwing in a small piece of bread which should sizzle). Take a spoonful of the *latke* mixture and lower carefully into the oil. Continue adding spoonfuls, not too close together, over the base of the pan.

*4* Flatten the pancakes slightly with the back of a spoon and after a few minutes when the *latkes* are golden brown on one side, carefully turn them over and continue frying until the other side is golden brown.

*5* Drain the *latkes* on kitchen paper and serve immediately.

# Aubergines with Garlic and Tomato Glaze

An unusual way of cooking aubergines, which tend to absorb large amounts of oil when fried. Roasting the slices in the oven makes them slightly crisp.

### INGREDIENTS

*Serves 4 as a side salad*
2 aubergines, about 225g/8oz each
2 garlic cloves
45ml/3 tbsp tomato purée
90–120ml/6–8 tbsp olive oil
2.5ml/½ tsp sugar
salt and ground black pepper
chopped flat leaf parsley, to garnish

> ── COOK'S TIP ──
>
> If the slices are very thin they tend to burn easily, so check after 15 minutes and move them around in the tin.

*1* Slice the aubergines about 5mm/¼in thick and spread them out on kitchen paper. Sprinkle with salt and leave for about 30 minutes. This will remove any bitter taste from the aubergines.

*2* Preheat the oven to 190°C/375°F/ Gas 5. Crush the garlic cloves and stir in the tomato purée, 15ml/1 tbsp oil and the seasoning. Pour about 60ml/4 tbsp oil into a baking tin.

*3* Rinse the aubergine slices in water, drain and dry them well. Arrange them over the oiled tin in a single layer. Spoon a little of the garlic tomato mixture over each one. Drizzle over the remaining oil and bake the slices for about 30 minutes.

*4* Carefully lift them off with a palette knife and arrange them, slightly overlapping, in a circle on a flat dish. Garnish with chopped parsley.

# Fresh Beetroot with Smatana

Freshly cooked summer beetroot have a brilliant colour and taste. They can also be made into a cold soup, *Borscht,* by grating the cooked beetroot and adding it to the cooking liquid with lemon juice and soured cream.

### INGREDIENTS

*Serves 4*
450g/1lb small uncooked beetroot
300ml/½ pint/1¼ cups creamed smatana (or soured cream)
salt and ground black pepper
dill sprigs, to garnish

*1* Cut off the leaves about 2.5cm/1in from the top of the beetroot and remove the thin roots at the other end. Wash the beetroot very well, removing any dirt with a vegetable brush.

*2* Cover the beetroot with water, season well, bring to the boil and simmer for about 30–40 minutes, or until they are soft. They are cooked when the skin peels off easily. Drain the beetroot, and when they have cooled slightly use a knife to peel off the skin.

*3* Spoon some of the chilled smatana on to individual plates, cut the beetroot into wedges and slide one of them over the smatana to make a pretty pink swirl. Arrange the rest of the quarters around the edge and garnish with dill sprigs.

# POULTRY

*With its crisp skin and dark flesh, duck is the most popular bird. Unless you can catch one, you won't see pigeon or quail on the table because kosher birds are never shot.*

*In Eastern Europe goose was a commonly eaten bird and the rendered fat was used for frying. Chicken fat, too, was used instead of butter to flavour potatoes and the famous chopped liver.*

*In our more health-conscious age, chicken and turkey are extremely popular and for cooking, most people use non-stick pans and a small amount of olive or sunflower oil. It is largely a matter of taste, so approximate quantities of oil are often given in the recipes.*

# Cold Sliced Roast Chicken

Cooking the chestnut stuffing under the skin keeps the breast meat succulent and creates a striped effect when carved.

## INGREDIENTS

*Serves 6–8 or more, as part of a buffet*
2 onions
30–45ml/2–3 tbsp oil
65g/2½ oz/1¼ cups fresh breadcrumbs
200g/7oz/¾ cups unsweetened
  chestnut purée
2kg/5lb fresh, free-range chicken
salt and ground black pepper
lettuce leaves and potatoes, to serve
flat leaf parsley, to garnish

*1* Chop one of the onions finely. Heat half of the oil in a small pan and sauté the onion until golden. Stir in 120ml/4fl oz/½ cup boiling water, take the pan off the heat and leave to stand for 5 minutes to absorb some of the liquid.

*2* Mix together the breadcrumbs, onion and chestnut purée with the onion and any liquid in the pan. Season well. Leave to cool completely.

*3* Preheat the oven to 220°C/425°F/ Gas 7. Wipe the chicken well with kitchen paper, inside and out, and carefully slide your hand under the skin on the breast to ease it away from the meat. Press the stuffing underneath the skin all over the breast.

*4* Brush a roasting tin with the remaining oil and put in the chicken, breast side down, with the remaining onion halves. Roast for 1 hour, basting occasionally and pouring away any excess.

*5* Turn the chicken over so that the breast is uppermost and continue to roast for a further 15 minutes, covering the top with a strip of foil if it looks too brown.

*6* When the chicken is cooked, leave it to cool before cutting downwards into slices. Serve with lettuce leaves and potatoes and garnish with flat leaf parsley.

# Golden Chicken

One of those rare dishes that is better cooked in advance and reheated. The chicken (preferably an old boiling one and not a young roaster) cooks in its own rich gravy. Leaving it to cool helps in the removal of any fat and improves the flavour.

## INGREDIENTS

*Serves 5–6*

15–30ml/1–2 tbsp oil
2.5kg/5½lb free-range chicken
30ml/2 tbsp plain flour
2.5ml/½ tsp paprika
600ml/1 pint/2½ cups boiling water
salt and ground black pepper
potatoes or rice, and broccoli, to serve

*1* Preheat the oven to 160°C/325°F/ Gas 3. Heat the oil in a large flameproof casserole and sauté the chicken slowly on all sides until the skin is brown. A boiling fowl is fatter so you should prick the skin with a fork on the back and legs to release the fat as the chicken cooks.

*2* Put the chicken on a plate and sprinkle the flour into the remaining oil, adding a little more if necessary to make a paste. Add the paprika and seasoning and slowly pour in the boiling water, stirring all the time to make a thick sauce. When the sauce is simmering, replace the chicken, spoon some of the sauce over the top and cover tightly with a sheet of foil and then the lid.

*3* Cook in the centre of the oven for about 1 hour and then turn the chicken over. Continue cooking for about 2 hours or until the chicken is tender (a roaster will cook far quicker than a boiler). Add a little extra boiling water if the sauce is drying up.

*4* When the meat on the legs is soft, the chicken is done. Leave to cool and pour the gravy into a bowl. When it is cold, chill in the fridge until the fat solidifies into a pale layer on the top. Remove with a spoon.

*5* Joint the chicken and pour over the cold gravy. Reheat until the gravy is very hot and serve with boiled potatoes or rice, and broccoli.

# Noodles with Aubergines and Chicken Livers

Noodle dough used to be made into little meat-filled pockets called *kreplach* which were served in soup. This modern pasta recipe has an unusual sauce.

## INGREDIENTS

*Serves 4*
**For the sauce**
2 large aubergines, about 350g/
   12oz each
2 garlic cloves
1 large onion
90–120ml/6–8 tbsp oil
500g/1¼ lb carton creamed tomatoes
250ml/8fl oz/1 cup boiling water
salt and ground black pepper
chopped flat leaf parsley, to garnish

**For the noodles**
675g/1½ lb flat noodles
275g/10oz chicken livers

*1* Peel and dice the aubergines. Sprinkle with salt and drain on kitchen paper for 30 minutes. Rinse and squeeze dry. Crush the garlic and chop the onion.

*2* Put half the oil in a frying pan and sauté the onion for about 1 minute. Add the garlic and cook until the onion starts to brown. Transfer to a plate and brown the aubergine in the remaining oil.

*3* Spoon over the onion, add the creamed tomatoes, boiling water and seasoning. Simmer for 30 minutes.

*4* Preheat the grill. Cook the noodles for 8 minutes. Meanwhile, grill the chicken livers on oiled foil for 3–4 minutes on each side. Snip into strips. Drain the noodles, spoon over the aubergine sauce and top with the chicken livers. Toss and serve, garnished with flat leaf parsley.

# Chicken with Pimientos

"Pimiento" is the Spanish word for pepper – a favourite ingredient in many Sephardi Mediterranean recipes.

## INGREDIENTS

*Serves 6*
2kg/5lb roasting chicken
1 large onion, sliced
2 garlic cloves, crushed
3 ripe tomatoes
2 large red peppers
60–90ml/4–6 tbsp olive oil
15ml/1 tbsp sugar
salt and ground black pepper
flat leaf parsley, to garnish

*1* Preheat the oven to 190°C/375°F/ Gas 5. Joint the chicken and cut into eight pieces and set aside. Skin and chop the tomatoes and seed and slice the red peppers.

*2* Heat half of the oil in a large frying pan and sauté the onion, garlic and peppers for 3 minutes. Transfer to an ovenproof dish and then fry the chicken pieces and add to the dish.

*3* Fry the tomatoes in the remaining oil for a few minutes. Add seasoning, sugar and 15ml/1 tbsp water, then spoon over the chicken. Cook uncovered in the oven for about 1 hour. Cover if the chicken is getting too brown. Half way through, pour the juices into a jug. Serve with black olives and boiled rice and garnish with parsley. Pour the fat off the juices in the jug and pass round as extra gravy.

# Chicken Pie with Mushrooms

The filling in this pie has an intense mushroom flavour, using chicken stock rather than the more usual milk and butter.

## INGREDIENTS

*Serves 4–6*
**For the pastry**
150g/5oz kosher margarine, chilled
225g/8oz/2 cups plain flour
1 egg yolk
60ml/4 tbsp cold water

**For the pie filling**
900g/2lb cooked roast or
　boiled chicken
45ml/3 tbsp olive oil
275g/10oz mixed dark mushrooms
　(flat, oyster or chestnut)
25ml/1½ tbsp flour
300ml/½ pint/1¼ cups chicken stock
15ml/1 tbsp soy sauce
1 egg white
salt and ground black pepper

*1* For the pastry, cut the margarine into small pieces and rub it into the flour until it is like breadcrumbs. Mix the egg yolk with the cold water and stir it into the flour mixture. Form the dough into a ball, cover and chill for about 30 minutes.

*2* Preheat the oven to 220°C/425°F/ Gas 7. For the filling, cut the cooked chicken into pieces and put them in a greased pie dish about 1.75 litres/3 pints/7½ cup capacity.

*3* Heat half the oil in a frying pan. Slice the mushrooms thickly and sauté them over high heat for about 3 minutes. Add the rest of the oil and stir in the flour. Season with pepper and slowly add the stock, stirring to make a thick sauce.

*4* Stir in the soy sauce, taste for seasoning and pour the mushroom sauce over the chicken. Roll out the pastry and cut one piece slightly larger than the size of the pie dish. Also cut some long strips about 2cm/³⁄₄ in wide. Place these round the rim of the pie dish, then lift the pastry on to the top, pressing it down on top of the strips. Knock up the edges with a knife.

*5* Lightly whisk the egg white and brush it over the pie. Bake in the oven for about 30–35 minutes.

--- COOK'S TIP ---

The pie can be made in advance up to Step 4 and chilled overnight or frozen. To cook from frozen leave at room temperature for a few hours and cook as above.

# Chicken Breasts with Burnt Almond Stuffing

Breadcrumbs are often used in stuffings, but this one is made from crunchy vegetables and matzo meal, so it is suitable for Passover.

## INGREDIENTS

*Serves 4*

4 fat spring onions
2 carrots
2 celery sticks
30ml/2 tbsp oil
60ml/4 tbsp flaked almonds
300ml/½ pint/1¼ cups chicken stock
   or 1 kosher chicken stock cube and
   boiling water
90ml/6 tbsp medium-ground
   matzo meal
4 chicken breasts with skin
salt and ground black pepper
dill sprigs, to garnish
mixed salad, to serve

---
COOK'S TIP

Freshly made chicken stock is always better than a stock cube but as this is a quick mid-week dish, the short-cut can be used.

---

*1* Preheat the oven to 190°C/375°F/ Gas 5. Slice the onions and chop the carrots and celery sticks into small pieces. Heat the oil in a frying pan and sauté the almonds until they are light brown. Remove with a slotted spoon and then sauté the chopped vegetables over medium heat for a few minutes.

*2* Add the seasoning, and pour in half of the stock. Cook over high heat until the liquid is slightly reduced and the vegetables are just moist. Mix in the matzo meal and the almonds.

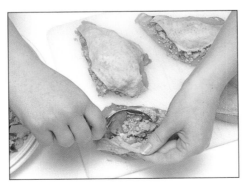

*3* Ease the skin off the chicken breasts on one side and press some of the stuffing underneath each one. Press the skin back over the stuffing and slash the skin to stop it curling up. Arrange the breasts in a roasting tin.

*4* Roast the chicken breasts, skin side up, for about 20–30 minutes or until the meat is tender and white. The skin should be crisp and brown.

*5* Keep the chicken warm while you make the gravy. Pour the remaining stock into the roasting tin and over medium heat stir in any chicken juices or bits of stuffing. Bring to the boil and then strain into a jug. Serve with a mixed salad and garnish with a dill sprig.

# Turkey Breasts with Wine and Grapes

Chicken and meat are never cooked with cream, so a good stock and wine provide the flavour in this velvety sauce.

### INGREDIENTS

*Serves 3*
450g/1lb turkey breast, thinly sliced
45ml/3 tbsp flour
45–90ml/3–4 tbsp oil
120ml/4fl oz/½ cup kosher white wine or sherry
120ml/4fl oz/½ cup chicken stock
150g/5oz white grapes
salt and ground black pepper
flat leaf parsley, to garnish
new potatoes or boiled rice, to serve (optional)

*1* Put the turkey slices in between sheets of greaseproof paper and flatten them with a rolling pin. Season the flour with salt and pepper and toss each turkey slice in it so that both sides are coated.

*2* Heat the oil in a large frying pan and sauté the turkey slices for about 3 minutes on each side. Pour in the wine or sherry and boil rapidly to reduce it slightly.

*3* Stir in the chicken stock, lower the heat and cook for another few minutes. Halve and seed the grapes and stir into the sauce. Serve with potatoes or rice, if using. Garnish with parsley.

---
COOK'S TIP

For a dark sauce you could use chestnut mushrooms. Sauté them in the oil before you cook the turkey as Step 2.

---

# Apple-stuffed Duck

Stuffing the duck breasts with whole apples keeps the slices moist and gives an attractive appearance when served cold.

### INGREDIENTS

*Serves 4, as a hot dish, more when served cold as part of a buffet*
40g/1½oz raisins or sultanas
30ml/2 tbsp kosher brandy
3 large onions
30ml/2 tbsp oil
175g/6oz fresh breadcrumbs
2 small apples, preferably cox
2 large duck breasts, including the skin
salt and ground black pepper
mixed leaf salad, to serve

*1* Soak the dried fruit in the brandy. Preheat the oven to 220°C/425°F/Gas 7.

*2* Chop one onion finely and sauté it in the oil until golden. Season with salt and pepper and add 50–120ml/2–4fl oz/¼–½ cup water. Bring to the boil and then add breadcrumbs until the stuffing is moist but not sloppy.

*3* Core and peel the apples. Drain the raisins and press them into the centre of the apples. Flatten the duck breasts and spread out, skin side down.

*4* Divide the stuffing between them and spread it over the meat. Place an apple at one end of each duck breast and carefully roll up to enclose the apples and stuffing. Secure with a length of cotton or fine string. Quarter the remaining onions. Prick the duck skin in several places to release the fat.

*5* Arrange on a rack in a roasting tin with the onions underneath. Roast for about 35 minutes. Pour off the fat and roast at 160°C/325°F/Gas 3 for a further 30–45 minutes.

*6* To serve cool, leave to get quite cold, chill and then cut each breast into 5 or 6 thin slices. Arrange on a platter and bring to room temperature before serving. Serve with a salad.

# DESSERTS

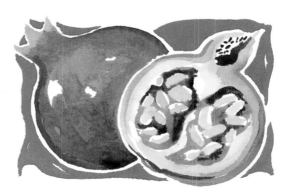

*Our grandparents would probably have ended a meal with a glass of lemon tea, some stewed fruit and a slice of sponge cake, called* plava.
*Cooks are more inventive today and have devised delicious dairy-free desserts, which are also light and more in line with current eating trends. The mounds of whipped cream that used to adorn trifles and gateaux have been replaced by fresh-tasting fruit sauces and sorbets. Cheesecake, often considered to be American, was almost certainly taken to the New World from Hungary.*
*Any pudding with cream is suitable to end a fish meal, but I have concentrated on pancakes, tarts and cakes where the emphasis is on fruit and berries. Lemon tea is still a good way to end a meal and for those who like a light fragrant drink, mint or jasmine tea are both refreshing.*

# Hazelnut Sponge Cake

A dessert for Passover, that does not contain any flour. The accompanying fruit coulis is good after a meat meal, and the vanilla sauce containing milk is suitable after a vegetarian or a fish main course.

## INGREDIENTS

6 large eggs, separated
175g/6oz/¾ cup caster sugar
juice and grated rind of 1 lemon
175g/6oz/¾ cup ground hazelnuts
25g/1oz fine-ground matzo meal
oil, for greasing

*1* Preheat the oven to 180°C/350°F/ Gas 4. Whisk the egg yolks with the sugar until the mixture is pale, thick and mousse-like. Add the juice and grated rind of the lemon.

*2* Whisk the egg whites until stiff. Add a quarter of the whisked whites to the yolk mixture and then fold in the hazelnuts, the matzo meal and the remaining whites. Take care not to deflate the mixture.

*3* Pour the mixture into a greased 25cm/10in cake tin and bake for 30–40 minutes. The centre should be dry when tested with a cocktail stick or thin skewer.

*4* When the cake is cool, take it out of the tin and store, covered, until ready for use. Serve it in wedges with Vanilla Sauce or Fruit Coulis.

# Fruit Coulis and Vanilla Sauce

These two sauces make a delicious combination or they can be served separately.

## INGREDIENTS

### For the fruit coulis
225g/8oz/1 cup blackberries or strawberries
30ml/2 tbsp caster sugar
15–30ml/1–2 tbsp water

### For the vanilla sauce
10ml/2 tsp potato flour
30ml/2 tbsp vanilla sugar
3 egg yolks (or 2 small eggs)
300ml/½ pint/1¼ cups milk

*1* For the coulis, put the berries in a pan with the sugar and water. Cook over low heat just until the berries collapse.

*2* Strain the fruit and juice through a nylon sieve into a jug.

*3* For the vanilla sauce, mix the potato flour, sugar and egg yolks to a paste. Add the cold milk.

*4* In a pan over low heat bring the mixture slowly to the boil, stirring. It will thicken after about 5 minutes. Take it off the heat, strain and cool. Serve with Hazelnut Sponge Cake.

— COOK'S TIP —

Store a cut vanilla pod in a jar of sugar. The sugar will absorb the vanilla flavour.

# Fruit Tree

A suitable pie for Tu B'Shvat, at the end of winter, when the almond trees blossom in Israel.

## INGREDIENTS

*Serves 4–6*

**For the pastry**
150g/5oz kosher margarine, chilled
225g/8oz/2 cups plain flour
1 egg, separated
60ml/4 tbsp cold water

**For the filling**
450g/1lb cooking apples, or fresh
  apricots or plums, stoned
60–120ml/4–8 tbsp sugar

*1* To make the pastry, rub the margarine into the flour until it is like breadcrumbs. Add the egg yolk and water, mix and form the dough into a ball. Cover and chill the dough for 30 minutes.

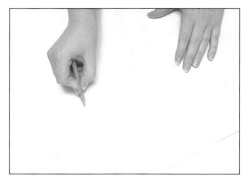

*2* Preheat the oven to 200°C/400°F/ Gas 6. Peel and core the apples or stone the summer fruit, if using. On a piece of paper, draw and cut out a tree shape about 30cm/12in high.

*3* Roll out the pastry and put the tree outline on top. Cut round the tree and then repeat, cutting a second tree about 1cm/½in larger.

*4* Lift the smaller shape on to a flat baking sheet. Cover with thinly-sliced apples, or the stoned fruit. Sprinkle over the sugar to taste, reserving 15ml/1 tbsp for the top.

*5* Cover the pie with the other tree outline, pressing it down at the edges. Whisk the egg white lightly and brush it all over the pie. Roll out the pastry trimmings and cut out some apple or plum shapes. Press these on to the tree and brush again with egg white. Sprinkle over the remaining sugar and bake for about 30–35 minutes.

*6* Slide a palette knife carefully underneath the tree and when it has cooled, transfer it to a large platter.

# Pear and Almond Flan with Chocolate Sauce

## INGREDIENTS

*Serves 4–6*

**For the flan**

225g/8oz kosher pastry
2 eggs, separated
50g/2oz/¼ cup caster sugar
50g/2oz/½ cup ground almonds
2 large comice or conference pears

**For the sauce**

115g/4oz plain dark chocolate
15ml/1 tbsp maple or golden syrup
30ml/2 tbsp hot water

*1* Roll out the pastry and use it to line a 20–25cm/8–10in flan tin. Preheat the oven to 200°C/400°F/ Gas 6. Bake blind by lining the pastry with greaseproof paper and baking beans or a double thickness of foil, for the first 10 minutes of cooking.

*2* Meanwhile, make the filling. Whisk the egg yolks with the sugar until pale and thick. Whisk the whites in a separate bowl. Fold the ground almonds into the yolk mixture and then fold in the whites.

*3* Peel and slice the pears. Take the pastry shell out of the oven, and turn the temperature down to 180°C/ 350°F/Gas 4. Remove the foil or beans and arrange the pears on the base. Spoon the almond mixture over the top, making sure the fruit is completely covered. Bake in the oven for about 15 minutes. The top will be slightly coloured and the almond mixture will be set.

*4* Make the sauce just before serving, otherwise it goes hard. Melt the chocolate in a bowl, either over simmering water or in the microwave for about 2 minutes. Stir in the syrup and hot water and mix until smooth.

*5* Serve the warm flan in portions, with a little of the chocolate sauce on the side.

# Charoset

Though sweet, Charoset is not really a dessert. It forms part of the symbolic feast (Seder service) held on the eve of Passover. Variations on this recipe go back for at least 2,000 years. Charoset is a finely chopped mixture which represents the mortar used by the Jewish slaves to make bricks in Egypt.

## INGREDIENTS

### Makes enough to fill a 350g/12oz jar
1 large cooking apple
75g/3oz/½ cup almonds, blanched and skinned
10ml/2 tsp ground cinnamon
30ml/2 tbsp kosher sweet red wine

*1* Peel, quarter and chop the apple. Chop it finely with the blanched almonds. If using a food processor make sure you don't process the mixture too finely, it should still be crunchy.

*2* Stir in the cinnamon and sweet wine and spoon the mixture into a jar. The colour and flavour develop after an hour or two.

*3* Serve as part of the Seder service or as a topping for matzah or matzo crackers.

---
VARIATIONS
---

This recipe is Ashkenazi, but Sephardim use a variety of other ingredients. Most common are dates, figs, sesame seeds, walnuts and raisins.

# Red Fruit Salad

Cut fruit usually deteriorates quickly but the juices from lightly-cooked mixed berries make a brilliant red coating, so this salad can be made the day before. It is also one of the quickest ways of making fruit salad for a crowd.

## INGREDIENTS

### Serves 8
225g/8oz/1 cup raspberries or blackberries
50g/2oz/¼ cup redcurrants or blackcurrants
30−60ml/2−4 tbsp sugar
8 ripe plums
8 ripe apricots
225g/8oz/1 cup seedless grapes
115g/4oz/½ cup strawberries

*1* Mix the berries and currants with 30ml/2 tbsp sugar. Stone the plums and apricots, cut them into pieces and put half of them into a pan with all of the berries.

*2* Cook over very low heat with about 45ml/3 tbsp water, or in a bowl with no water, in the microwave, until the fruit is just beginning to soften and the juices are starting to run.

*3* Leave to cool slightly and then add the reserved plums and apricots, and the grapes. Taste for sweetness and add more sugar if the fruit is too tart. Leave the fruit salad to cool, cover and chill − overnight if necessary.

*4* Just before serving, transfer the fruit to a serving bowl. Slice the strawberries and arrange them over the fruit in the bowl.

# Lemon Mousse

A mousse without cream but with the tangy taste of lemons.

## Ingredients

*Serves 8*
15ml/1 tbsp kosher gelatine
juice and grated zest of
    4 unwaxed lemons
6 large eggs, separated
175g/6oz/scant cup caster sugar

---
— Cook's Tip —

It is important to add hot gelatine to a hot mixture or cool gelatine to a cool one, otherwise it becomes stringy.

---

*1* Sprinkle the gelatine into a cup and add about 120ml/4fl oz/½ cup lemon juice. Stir and leave for a minute to swell. Stand the cup in a little simmering water in the bottom of a saucepan and stir until the gelatine melts. It will be almost clear and quite thin. Take the cup out of the pan.

*2* Whisk the egg yolks with 150g/ 5oz/¾ cup sugar until the mixture is thick and very pale. Spoon it into the top part of a double saucepan (or a bowl set over a pan of simmering water). Add 15ml/1 tbsp lemon zest and the remaining lemon juice. Stir the mixture constantly until it begins to thicken.

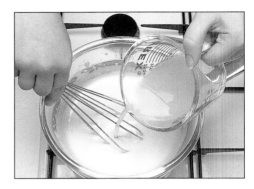

*3* After about 5 minutes the mixture should be thick and warm. Test the temperature with your finger as it should be as hot as the gelatine. Pour the gelatine into the lemon mixture and stir for a couple of minutes.

*4* Take the pan (or bowl) off the hot water and cool it quickly. Leave until cool, but not too cold.

*5* Whisk the egg whites and when they begin to stiffen, add the remaining 30ml/2 tbsp sugar. Gently fold them into the lemon yolk mixture.

*6* Pour the mousse into a glass bowl and decorate with lemon zest. Chill or freeze.

# Pancakes with Fruit

Milk is usually a prominent ingredient in crêpes but you can make thin pancakes with fresh orange juice instead.

## INGREDIENTS

*Makes about 12*

115g/4oz/1 cup plain flour
pinch of salt
1 beaten egg
150ml/¼ pint/⅔ cup fresh orange juice
150ml/¼ pint/⅔ cup iced water
oil, for frying
mint leaves, to decorate
strawberries, sliced peaches and orange
  segments, to serve

*1* Sift the flour and salt into a bowl. In another bowl, beat together the egg, orange juice and water.

*2* Make a well in the centre of the flour and gradually beat in some of the egg mixture, stirring well to get rid of any lumps. Continue adding the liquid until you have a smooth batter. Chill for at least 30 minutes.

*3* Pour a little oil into a small frying pan and turn on the heat. Then pour it back into a jug, leaving just a film on the bottom of the pan. When this is hot, pour in enough batter to thinly cover the base.

*4* Slide a palette knife around the edge and under the pancake and then turn it over. It should be golden. Cook the other side for about a minute so that both sides are light brown.

*5* Continue cooking the rest of the mixture until all the batter is used. Serve with fresh fruit.

--- COOK'S TIP ---

You can make the pancakes in advance, stack them in between sheets of grease-proof paper when they are cool, store them in the fridge or freezer.

# Cheesecake with Berries

Bought cheesecakes can be very sweet; this one is light and fresh.

### INGREDIENTS

*Serves 6–8*
225g/8oz digestive biscuits
75g/3oz butter
5 eggs, separated
150g/5oz/²/₃ cup caster sugar or
  vanilla sugar
450g/1lb/2 cups curd or ricotta cheese
175ml/6fl oz/ ¾ cup soured cream
5ml/1 tsp vanilla essence (optional)
30ml/2 tbsp self-raising flour, sifted
raspberries and blueberries, to serve
mint leaves, to decorate

*1* Preheat the oven to 140°C/275°F/ Gas 1. Crush the biscuits finely and melt the butter in a pan over low heat. Mix the crumbs with the melted butter and press the mixture over the base and slightly up the sides of a loose-bottomed 20cm/8in cake tin.

*2* Beat the egg yolks with the sugar and when they are pale and thick, add the curd cheese. Stir in the soured cream and vanilla essence, if using.

*3* Whisk the egg whites until stiff and fold them in with the flour. Spoon the mixture into the prepared cake tin and bake for 45 minutes. Turn the oven off and leave for a further hour without opening the oven door.

*4* Take the cake out and leave it to cool completely in the tin. Remove and serve cool, but not chilled, with fresh berries. Decorate with mint leaves.

# Haman's Ears

These crisp lightly-sugared pastries are eaten on the Festival of Purim. Shaped like ears, the thin dough puffs up when fried. It is impossible to eat just one!

### INGREDIENTS

*Makes about 20 thin pastries*
115g/4oz/1 cup flour
2.5ml/½ tsp baking powder
1 egg
30ml/2 tbsp water
few drops orange flower water
oil, for frying
icing sugar, to decorate

*1* Sift together the flour and baking powder and make a well in the centre. Drop in the egg and add the water and orange flower water. Stir until the mixture forms a dough.

*2* Roll out on a lightly floured board, sprinkling the pin with flour to prevent sticking. When very thin, cut into 10cm/4in rounds. Re-roll the trimmings and use to cut more rounds.

*3* Cut the circles in half, squeezing the centres slightly to make ear-shapes. Heat some oil in a deep pan and fry the ears, a few at a time, until they are golden brown. It only takes a few minutes.

*4* Drain the pastries on kitchen paper and sprinkle with sifted icing sugar. They will be quite dry and not at all oily. Serve cold with tea or coffee.

# BREADS, CAKES AND PASTRIES

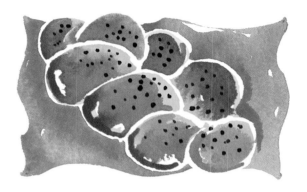

When coarse brown bread was considered everyday food, the special plaited loaves always had to be made of fine white flour. So even though it is fashionable to eat dark nutty breads today, the sweet white challah has remained unchanged.

A family's origins are often reflected in the cakes and pastries served at their parties. Hand-made individual pastries like ma-amoul come from Egypt; apple pie or strudel from Austria. The most authentic of all Jewish cakes are those baked for Passover (with no flour or baking powder) and honey cake, served at New Year. Each slice carries with it hopes of a sweet year to come.

# Challah

Plaited *challah* loaves are served at the Sabbath meals.

### INGREDIENTS

*Makes 2 loaves*
450g/1lb/4 cups strong white flour
7.5ml/1½ tsp salt
10ml/2 tsp caster sugar (optional)
10ml/2 tsp quick-acting dried yeast
45ml/3 tbsp oil
250ml/8fl oz/1 cup warm water
2 eggs
poppy seeds, to decorate

*1* Sift together the flour, salt and sugar, if using, and sprinkle over the yeast. Mix the oil, half of the water and 1 egg. The water must be warm; if too hot or too cold, the bread won't rise. Add the remaining water to the flour and then the oil and egg mixture.

*2* Mix together until a dough is formed, then knead until smooth and elastic, using a little extra flour if it seems sticky.

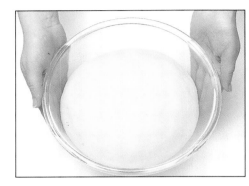

*3* Put the dough in a greased bowl, cover with a clean dish towel and leave in a warm place for at least 2 hours or until doubled in size. Knock back the dough by kneading it again and then divide it into two.

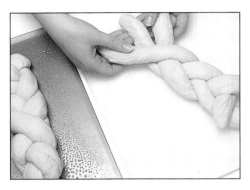

*4* Cut each piece into three and roll them into long sausage shapes. Using three strands for each loaf, plait the dough and push the ends underneath. Leave to rise on an oiled baking sheet for about 30 minutes.

*5* Preheat the oven to 220°C/425°F/ Gas 7. Brush the loaves with egg, sprinkle with poppy seeds and bake for about 35 minutes. Cool on a wire tray.

# Date Bread

Dates go back to biblical times. Dried fruits have a natural sweetness so this loaf needs no added sugar.

### INGREDIENTS

*Makes 1 loaf – about 16 slices*
225g/8oz/1⅓ cups dried
   dates, chopped
2.5ml/½ tsp bicarbonate of soda
150ml/¼ pint/⅔ cup boiling water
1 egg
15g/½oz butter, softened
150g/5oz/⅔ cup self-raising flour
lightly salted butter, to serve

---
##### COOK'S TIP

Date bread keeps well for a few days wrapped in foil. To freeze, wrap in clear film. Defrost for two hours before use.

---

*1* Preheat the oven to 160°C/325°F/ Gas 3. Put the dried dates in a bowl with the bicarbonate of soda and boiling water. Leave the dates to soak for about 5 minutes.

*2* Grease and line a 450g/1lb loaf tin with buttered greaseproof paper so that it comes to at least 2.5cm/1in above the tin.

*3* Stir the egg, butter and flour into the date mixture and beat until smooth. The small pieces of date give the bread texture. Pour the mixture into the prepared tin.

*4* Bake for about 1 hour in the centre of the oven. Test with a strand of raw spaghetti or a thin skewer. When the bread is cool, take it out of the tin and remove the paper. Serve sliced and buttered.

# Cinnamon Rolls

## INGREDIENTS

*Makes 24 small rolls*

**For the dough**

400g/14oz/1²/₃ cups strong white flour
2.5ml/½ tsp salt
30ml/2 tbsp sugar
5ml/1 tsp quick-acting dried yeast
45ml/3 tbsp oil
1 egg
120ml/4fl oz/½ cup warm milk
120ml/4fl oz/½ cup warm water

**For the filling**

25g/1oz butter, softened
25g/1oz dark brown sugar
2.5–5ml/½–1 tsp ground cinnamon
15ml/1 tbsp raisins or sultanas

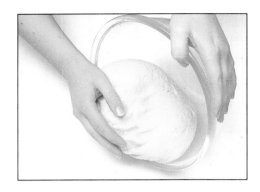

*1* Sift the flour, salt and sugar and sprinkle over the yeast. Mix the oil, egg, milk and water and add to the flour. Mix to a dough, then knead until smooth. Leave to rise until doubled in size and then knock it back again.

*2* Roll out the dough into a large rectangle and cut in half vertically. Spread over the soft butter, reserving 15ml/1 tbsp for brushing. Mix the sugar and cinnamon and sprinkle over the top. Dot with the raisins.

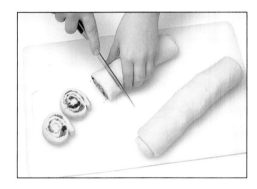

*3* Roll each piece into a long Swiss roll shape, to enclose the filling. Cut into 2.5cm/1in slices, arrange flat on a greased baking sheet and brush with the remaining butter. Leave to prove again for about 30 minutes.

*4* Preheat the oven to 200°C/400°F/ Gas 6 and bake the cinnamon rolls for about 20 minutes. Leave to cool on a wire rack. Serve fresh for breakfast or tea, with extra butter if liked.

# Peach Kuchen

The joy of this cake is its all-in-one simplicity. It can be served straight from the oven, or cut into squares when cold.

## INGREDIENTS

*Serves 8*

350g/12oz/3 cups self-raising flour
225g/8oz/1 cup caster sugar
175g/6oz/³⁄₄ cup unsalted
    butter, softened
2 eggs
120ml/4fl oz/½ cup milk
6 large peeled peaches, sliced or
    450g/1lb plums or cherries, stoned
115g/4oz/½ cup soft brown sugar
2.5ml/½ tsp ground cinnamon
soured cream or crème fraîche,
    to serve (optional)

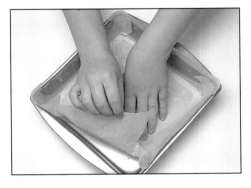

*1* Preheat the oven to 190°C/375°F/ Gas 5. Grease and line a 20 x 25 x 2.5cm/8 x 10 x 1in cake tin.

*2* Put the flour, sugar, butter, eggs and milk into a large bowl and beat for a few minutes until you have a smooth batter. Spoon it into the prepared cake tin.

*3* Arrange the peaches, plums or cherries over the cake mixture. Mix the brown sugar and cinnamon and sprinkle over the fruit.

---
COOK'S TIP
---

To skin ripe peaches, cover with boiling water for 20 seconds. The skin will then slip off easily.

*4* Bake for about 40 minutes, testing for doneness by inserting a cocktail stick in the centre.

*5* Serve the cake warm or cool with the soured cream or crème fraîche, if using.

# Chocolate Brownies

The American versions of this recipe are usually rich in fat. The no-butter version still tastes dark and gooey, but is best eaten on the day it is made.

**INGREDIENTS**

*Makes about 20*
120ml/4fl oz/½ cup sunflower oil
150g/5oz plain dark chocolate
2 eggs
115g/4oz/1 cup self-raising flour
115g/4oz/½ cup caster sugar
5ml/1 tsp vanilla essence
75g/3oz/1 cup halved pecan nuts

*1* Preheat the oven to 200°C/400°F/ Gas 6. Use a little of the oil to grease a 23cm/9in square shallow cake tin and line it with lightly oiled greaseproof paper.

*2* Melt the chocolate with the remaining oil in a bowl over simmering water

---
COOK'S TIP

The easiest way to melt ingredients is in the microwave. To soften chocolate, butter, sugar or syrup, microwave on full power for a few minutes or until soft.

---

*3* Beat the eggs lightly and add them to the chocolate, stirring vigorously. Beat in the flour, sugar and vanilla essence and pour the mixture into the tin. Arrange the pecans over the top.

*4* Bake for about 10–15 minutes. If you like chewy brownies, take them out of the oven now. If you want a more cake-like finish, leave for another 5 minutes. Cut into squares and cool before removing from the tin.

---

# Honey Cake

The honey in this cake can be replaced by golden syrup, but it needs natural brown sugar and ginger to give it the characteristic taste and colour.

**INGREDIENTS**

75g/3oz/6 tbsp unsalted butter
75g/3oz/6 tbsp molasses or dark brown sugar
75ml/5 tbsp honey or golden syrup
225g/8oz/2 cups self-raising flour
1.5ml/¼ tsp bicarbonate of soda
5ml/1 tsp ground ginger
150ml/¼ pint/⅔ cup milk
1 egg

*1* Preheat the oven to 180°C/350°F/ Gas 4. Grease and line a 450g/1lb loaf tin with a sheet of buttered greaseproof paper.

*2* Melt the butter, sugar and honey in a pan over very low heat, stirring constantly. Don't let the mixture boil.

*3* Sift together the flour, bicarbonate of soda and ginger and stir in the milk and egg. Pour the honey mixture into the dry ingredients and beat well until smooth.

*4* Pour into the prepared tin and bake in the oven for about 45 minutes. The cake will rise and should be dry in the middle when tested with a strand of raw spaghetti or thin skewer.

*5* Cool on a wire rack and then wrap the cake in foil. The flavour actually improves after a day.

# Coconut Pyramids

Coconut biscuits are sold in Israeli street markets during Passover.

### INGREDIENTS

*Makes about 15*

225g/8oz/1 cup unsweetened desiccated coconut
115g/4oz/½ cup caster sugar
2 egg whites
oil, for greasing

— COOK'S TIP —

To freeze biscuits, arrange in a single layer on a tray. When hard, pack in bags or boxes. Defrost for 1 hour before use.

*1* Preheat the oven to 190°C/375°F/ Gas 5. Grease a large baking sheet with a little oil.

*2* Mix together the desiccated coconut and the sugar. Lightly whisk the egg whites. Fold enough egg white into the coconut to make a fairly firm mixture. You may not need quite all the egg whites.

*3* Form the mixture into pyramid shapes by taking a teaspoonful and rolling it first into a ball. Flatten the base and press the top into a point. Arrange the pyramids on the baking sheet, leaving a space between them.

*4* Bake for 12–15 minutes on a low shelf. The tips should begin to turn golden and the pyramids should be just firm, but still soft inside.

*5* Slide a palette knife under the pyramids to loosen them, and leave to cool before removing from the baking sheet.

# Cinnamon Balls

Ground almonds or hazelnuts form the basis of most Passover cakes and biscuits. These balls should be soft inside, with a very strong cinnamon flavour. They harden with keeping, so it is a good idea to freeze some and only use them when required.

## INGREDIENTS

*Makes about 15*

175g/6oz/ 1¹/₂ cups ground almonds
75g/3oz/¹/₃ cup caster sugar
15ml/1 tbsp ground cinnamon
2 egg whites
oil, for greasing
icing sugar, for dredging

*1* Preheat the oven to 180°C/350°F/ Gas 4. Grease a large baking sheet with oil.

*2* Mix together the ground almonds, sugar and cinnamon. Whisk the egg whites until they begin to stiffen and fold enough into the almonds to make a fairly firm mixture.

*3* Wet your hands with cold water and roll small spoonfuls of the mixture into balls. Place these at intervals on the baking sheet.

*4* Bake for about 15 minutes in the centre of the oven. They should be slightly soft inside – too much cooking will make them hard and tough.

*5* Slide a palette knife under the balls to release them from the baking sheet and leave to cool. Sift a few tablespoons of icing sugar on to a plate and when the cinnamon balls are cold slide them on to the plate. Shake gently to completely cover the cinnamon balls in sugar and store in an airtight container or in the freezer.

# Chocolate Apricots

Something to nibble with after-dinner coffee, these are simple and quick to make, but be certain to use the best quality chocolate rather than "chocolate flavour coating".

## INGREDIENTS

*Makes about 24*
50g/2oz plain chocolate
12 large dried apricots

---
COOK'S TIP
---

To melt this quantity of chocolate in the microwave, put it on a plate and cook on HIGH for about 1 minute.

*1* Take a length of foil and line a baking sheet with it.

*2* Melt the chocolate in a small bowl over simmering water.

*3* Cut each apricot into 2–3 strips. Dip the long cut side of each strip into the melted chocolate and immediately place it on the foil. Put the tray of chocolate apricots in the freezer for about 30 minutes.

*4* Slide the apricots off the foil by pressing from underneath and store them in a covered container in the fridge or the freezer. To defrost, arrange on a plate and leave for 30 minutes.

# Baklava

Sweet syrup-soaked pastries are popular in Greece and the Middle East. This version is flavoured with lemon and rose water.

## INGREDIENTS

*Makes about 30*
200g/7oz/large cup shelled pistachio nuts
5ml/1 tsp caster sugar
10ml/2 tsp rose water
270g/10oz filo pastry
50ml/2fl oz/¼ cup oil

### For the syrup
175ml/6fl oz/ ¾ cup water
300g/11oz/1½ cups caster sugar
juice of 1 lemon

*1* Chop the pistachio nuts in a food processor. Don't grind them too finely. Stir in the sugar and rose water.

*2* Preheat the oven to 180°C/350°F/Gas 4. Cut the sheets of filo pastry in half. Brush a little oil on to the base and sides of a 25cm/10in square baking tin. Put in a sheet of pastry, brush with oil and cover with a second sheet. Use up half of the pastry this way.

*3* Spread the nut mixture over the pastry and cover with a filo sheet. Repeat until oil and pastry are used up.

*4* Using a sharp knife, cut vertical lines 4cm/1½in apart. Cut right through the pastry and nuts, then cut diagonal lines to form diamond shapes. Bake in the centre of the oven for 15–20 minutes.

*5* To make the syrup, put the water and sugar in a small pan and heat slowly. Stir once or twice and when it boils add 30ml/2 tbsp lemon juice. Boil the syrup for about 6 minutes. Stir in the remaining lemon juice and leave to cool and thicken slightly.

*7* After 20 minutes turn the oven temperature to 150°C/300°F/Gas 2 and cook the baklava for another 20 minutes. Cool for about 10 minutes.

*8* Pour the syrup over the baklava. Leave for several hours or overnight.

# Ma-amoul – Date-filled Pastries

From Gibraltar to Baghdad women would get together to make hundreds of these labour-intensive pastries. Making a small quantity is not so lengthy.

## INGREDIENTS

*Makes about 25*
175g/6oz/1½ cups plain flour
75g/3oz/6 tbsp margarine or butter, softened
5ml/1 tsp rose water
5ml/1 tsp orange flower water
45ml/3 tbsp water

**For the filling**
115g/4oz/⅔ cup stoned dried dates
2.5ml/½ tsp orange flower water
20ml/4 tsp sifted icing sugar, for sprinkling

*1* To make the filling, chop the dates finely. Add 50ml/2fl oz/¼ cup boiling water and the orange flower water, beat the mixture vigorously and leave to cool.

*2* To make the pastries, rub the margarine or butter into the flour. Add the rose and orange flower waters and the water and mix to a firm dough.

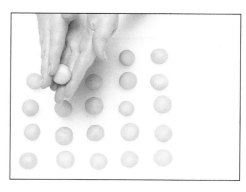

*3* Shape the dough into about 25 small balls.

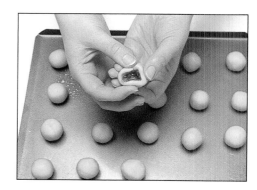

*4* Preheat the oven to 180°C/350°F/Gas 4. Press your finger into each ball to make a small container, pressing the sides round and round to make the walls thinner. Put about 1.5ml/¼ tsp of the date mixture into each one and seal by pressing the pastry together.

*5* Arrange the date pastries, seam side down, on a lightly greased baking sheet and prick each one with a fork. Bake for 15–20 minutes and cool.

*6* Put the cooled pastries on a plate and sprinkle over the icing sugar. Shake lightly to make sure they are covered. Date Ma-amoul freeze well.

---
COOK'S TIP
---

The secret of good Ma-amoul is to get as much date filling into the pastry as possible, but you must make sure to seal the opening well. The traditional way to decorate them was to make a pattern using tweezers, but it is quicker to use a fork.

# Flaked Almond Biscuits

It is always useful to have a jar of crisp home-made biscuits to offer to friends.

## INGREDIENTS

*Makes about 30*
175g/6oz/¾ cup butter or
   kosher margarine
225g/8oz/2 cups self-raising flour, plus
   extra for dusting
150g/5oz/¾ cup caster sugar
2.5ml/½ tsp ground cinnamon
1 egg, separated
30ml/2 tbsp cold water
50g/2oz/½ cup flaked almonds

*1* Preheat the oven to 180°C/350°F/ Gas 4. Rub the butter or margarine into the flour. Reserve 15ml/1 tbsp sugar and mix the rest with the cinnamon. Stir into the flour and then add the egg yolk and cold water and mix to a firm paste.

*2* Roll the dough out on a lightly floured board and when 1cm/½in thick, sprinkle over the almonds. Continue rolling, pressing the almonds into the dough so that it is about 5mm/¼in thick.

*3* Using a fluted round cutter, cut the dough into rounds. Use a palette knife to lift them on to an ungreased baking sheet. You can re-form the dough and cut more rounds to use it all up. Whisk the white of the egg lightly, brush it over the biscuits, and sprinkle over the remaining sugar.

*4* Bake in the centre of the oven for about 10–15 minutes or until golden. To remove, slide a palette knife under the biscuits, which will still seem a bit soft, but they harden as they cool. Leave on a wire rack until quite cold. Store the almond biscuits in an airtight container.

# Index